GOD
& His Church

THE ANGLO-CATHOLIC
CONGRESS BOOKS

VOLUME ONE

Books 1—16

WIPF & STOCK · Eugene, Oregon

Also published for the
Anglo-Catholic Congress:

The Anglo-Catholic Book of Prayers

Catholic and Evangelical Addresses
W. J. SEXTON

The Report of the First Anglo-Catholic Priests' Convention

The Report of the Anglo-Catholic Congress, London, 1923

Wipf and Stock Publishers
199 W 8th Ave, Suite 3
Eugene, OR 97401

God and His Church
The Anglo-Catholic Congress Books, Volume 1, Books 1-16
By Prestige, George Leonard
ISBN 13: 978-1-5326-7839-4
Publication date 12/26/2018
Previously published by The Society of SS. Peter & Paul, Ltd., 1923

THE CONGRESS BOOKS
General Editor:
LEONARD PRESTIGE, B.D.
Rector of Upper Heyford, Oxon.

1. IS THERE A GOD? By Canon A. R. WHITHAM, Principal of Culham College.
2. IS THERE A TRUE RELIGION? By A. E. J. RAWLINSON, Student of Christ Church, Oxford.
3. THE DOCTRINE OF THE TRINITY. By PETER GREEN, Canon of Manchester, Chaplain to the King.
4. THE DEITY OF CHRIST. By N. P. WILLIAMS, Fellow of Exeter College, Oxford.
5. THE VIRGIN BIRTH. By C. B. MOSS, Assistant Priest of St. Bartholomew's, Dublin.
6. THE RESURRECTION OF CHRIST. By B. T. D. SMITH, Fellow of Sidney Sussex College, Cambridge.
7. THE ASCENSION. By F. W. GREEN, Fellow of Merton College, Oxford.
8. THE HOLY GHOST. By G. C. JOYCE, D.D., Canon of St. Asaph, late Principal of St. David's College, Lampeter.
9. MIRACLES. By ARTHUR CHANDLER, D.D., late Bishop of Bloemfontein.

10. A SIMPLE LIFE OF OUR LORD. By LEONARD PRESTIGE, Rector of Upper Heyford, Oxon.
11. A SHORT HISTORY OF THE CATHOLIC CHURCH. By W. H. HUTTON, D.D., Dean of Winchester.
12. CHRIST AND CATHOLICISM. By CLEMENT HOSKYNS, Fellow of Corpus Christi College, Cambridge.
13. THE AUTHORITY OF THE CHURCH. By LEIGHTON PULLAN, D.D., Fellow of St. John's College, Oxford.
14. THE USE OF CREEDS. By F. H. BRABANT, Fellow of Wadham College, Oxford.
15. ENGLISH CATHOLICISM AND THE SEE OF ROME. By A. F. HOOD, Librarian of Pusey House, Oxford.
16. ANGLO-CATHOLICISM. By M. E. ATLAY, late Vicar of St. Matthew's, Westminster.

17. THE OLD TESTAMENT. By Preb. E. J. BICKNELL, Vice-Principal of Cuddesdon College.
18. THE NEW TESTAMENT. By Preb. E. J. BICKNELL.
19. THE BIBLE AS THE WORD OF GOD. By J. C. H. HOW, Superior, O.G.S.
20. THE CHRISTIAN MORAL IDEAL. By K. E. KIRK, Fellow of Trinity College, Oxford.
21. OTHERWORLDLINESS AND SOCIAL REFORM. By FRANCIS UNDERHILL, Vicar of St. Mary and St. John, Oxford.
22. HUMAN MIND AND WILL. By Professor A. E. TAYLOR, St. Andrews.

THE CONGRESS BOOKS, *Continued*

23 **SEX-INSTRUCTION.** By MARY SCHARLIEB, M.D.

24 **THE MEANING OF SACRAMENTS.** By CHARLES HARRIS, D.D., Rector of Colwall.
25 **EUCHARISTIC WORSHIP.** By M. R. NEWBOLT, Perpetual Curate of St. Michael's, Brighton.
26 **THE SACRIFICE OF THE MASS.** By S. R. P. MOULSDALE, Principal of St. Chad's College, Durham.
27 **HOLY COMMUNION.** By J. F. BRISCOE, Rector of Bagborough, Somerset.
28 **RESERVATION OF THE BLESSED SACRAMENT.** By Canon DARWELL STONE, D.D., Principal of Pusey House, Oxford.
29 **CEREMONIAL.** By MAURICE CHILD, Librarian of Pusey House, Oxford.

30 **BAPTISM AND CONFIRMATION.** By L. S. THORNTON, C.R.
31 **CONFESSION AND ABSOLUTION.** By Fr. VERNON, S.D.C.
32 **MARRIAGE ; ORDERS ; AND UNCTION.** By B. W. RANDOLPH, D.D., Canon of Ely.
33 **APOSTOLIC SUCCESSION.** By C. H. TURNER, F.B.A., Ireland Professor, Oxford.
34 **EPISCOPACY.** By LEONARD PRESTIGE, Rector of Upper Heyford, Oxon.
35 **SACERDOTALISM EXPLAINED.** By E. M. MILNER-WHITE, Fellow of King's College, Cambridge.
36 **SACERDOTALISM IN THE PRIMITIVE CHURCH.** By Canon W. J. SPARROW SIMPSON, D.D., Chaplain of St. Mary's Hospital, Ilford.

37 **EVOLUTION AND THE FALL.** By E. O. JAMES, D.Litt., F.S.A., F.R.A.I., Vicar of St. Thomas', Oxford.
38 **WHAT IS WRONG WITH MAN?** By Canon J. B. SEATON, Principal of Cuddesdon College.
39 **SIN : DOES IT MATTER?** By ARTHUR MONTFORD Vicar of the Church of the Ascension, Lavender Hill.
40 **THE ATONEMENT.** By J. K. MOZLEY, Principal of Leeds Clergy School.
41 **CONVERSION.** By H. P. BULL, Superior-General, S.S.J.E.
42 **FAITH AND WORKS.** By Preb. L. A. PHILLIPS, Principal of Lichfield Theological College.
43 **VOCAL PRAYER.** By G. W. HOCKLEY, Rector of Liverpool.
44 **MENTAL PRAYER.** By M. R. CARPENTER-GARNIER, Librarian of Pusey House, Oxford.
45 **CHRISTIAN ASCETICISM.** By ARTHUR CHANDLER, D.D., late Bishop of Bloemfontein.
46 **MONASTICISM.** By H. NORTHCOTT, C.R.

47 **MARY AND THE SAINTS.** By H. F. KIRKPATRICK, Principal of Dorchester Missionary College.
48 **INVOCATION OF SAINTS.** By G. H. CLAYTON, Fellow of Peterhouse and Vicar of St. Mary-the-less, Cambridge.
49 **HEAVEN.** By E. GRAHAM, Fellow of Oriel College, Oxford.
50 **HELL.** By DAVID JENKS, S.S.M.
51 **PURGATORY.** By Canon DARWELL STONE, D.D., Principal of Pusey House, Oxford.
52 **THE END OF THE WORLD.** By T. A. LACEY, Canon of Worcester.

Published by the Society of SS. Peter & Paul, Limited

THE CONGRESS BOOKS: No. 1

IS THERE A GOD?

A. R. WHITHAM
Principal of Culham College,
Hon. Canon of Christ Church

LONDON
THE SOCIETY OF
SS. PETER & PAUL
32 George St., Hanover Sq., W. 1, *and*
The Abbey House, Westminster, S.W. 1

Is There a God?

MOST of us were first told of the existence of God by our parents and we accepted it on their authority. But later on we discovered that behind their statement lay a long tradition of human belief. In all times and in all countries the vast majority of mankind have believed in the existence of some divine person or persons, who had some connexion with themselves and their own lives.

It is true that the forms which this belief has taken have been almost infinitely varied. They have ranged from the shuddering superstitions of the savage to the austere and splendid monotheism of the Hebrew prophets; from the dread of malevolent deities who must be propitiated by grotesque charms or cruel sacrifices, to the Christian's glowing thought of a universal Father, whose very nature is love. But beyond this bewildering variety, the fact remains that there is a continuous and practically universal tradition, which seems to be inherent in human nature. This fact claims at least consideration and the weighing of evidence.

We ask then, first, does the world itself

4 Signs of a Personal God

this material universe which surrounds us, offer any evidence for the existence of God? Clearly the world demands some explanation. How did it come to be? Why is it what it is—a system of ordered law, in which events follow from causes, in which calculations are possible? Or, again, what is the secret of the age-long progress which has led from the lowest forms of life to the birth of man?

The magic word 'evolution' is in itself no answer to these questions about the natural world. It is only a convenient description of the apparent course of events. Evolution cannot explain the laws of nature, nor can it explain origins. Granted that the earth, the sun, the stars move in fixed and calculable courses, where did the first impact come from that launched them on their way? Granted that all the life on this planet developed from a single cell of protoplasm, where and how was that produced? No explanation seems possible except that of some originating will.

Nor is it merely these beginnings of things that suggest some personal intervention. All the life of the world in all its forms and developments must have been contained implicitly in that primordial cell, as the tree is contained in the single seed. The whole process of evolution postulates some scheme, some directing purpose. And schemes and purposes, like origins, can only proceed from personal thought and personal will.

Signs of a Personal God

The contemplation of the world, therefore, convinces me that there is some rational basis for it all; that it is the work of a mind which corresponds to my own mind; that it was originated and is being shaped under some rational guidance and to some rational end. Otherwise no science would be possible.

Yet the universe is not merely an established order, whose laws my mind can grasp, and to some extent utilize. Nor does it merely suggest to me an indwelling intelligence, a directing will. The universe is beautiful. It is a spectacle—or rather, an unending series of new spectacles—of beauty, beauty eternally varied, of which no physical explanation can be given; beauty of the sunset, of the ever-changing sea, of the starry heavens, the blossoming earth, the mountains and the meadows, the birds, the beasts, the face of man.

And all this, while it entrances us with its charm, and elevates and purifies our thoughts, yet serves no tangible or material purpose. Evolution can tell us nothing of the origin or meaning of natural beauty. It is the outstanding riddle of the materialist. I can conceive no explanation of it unless it be the effect of the living imagination and delight of a great master-artist, who rejoices in every aspect of his work, and moment by moment devises new combinations of light and colour and shape and harmony.

6 Is this God a Moral Being?

THOUGHT, will, purpose, imagination, all these are attributes of a personal being; they have no meaning except in connexion with personality. The universe bears the mark of them all. So far the only explanation of them appears to lie in the truth of the human tradition, that there is a God. Many would go with us as far as this, but hesitate to go further. And yet we must go further, if our conception of God is to be anything more to us than a far-off mystery and wonder. Is there any evidence that this Spirit of the universe is a moral being, to whom Justice and Right and Love mean the same that they do to us?

Looking within ourselves we recognize the fact of conscience. However this mysterious sense may have developed, however varying its mandates may be in different stages of human life, the fact remains that there it is. I cannot deny the existence of conscience in myself. I may defy it, or smother it, but I cannot evade it altogether. There is this supreme 'ought' to be reckoned with, as insistent in its own sphere as the laws of mathematics are in theirs. It cannot be explained away as the inherited or instinctive deference to the customs and regulations of human society. For conscience is sometimes admitted to reach its highest and noblest expression, its most undeniable rightness,

Is this God a Moral Being? 7

when it defies human conventions and traditions. And I can find no justification for conscience except it be the reflection in myself of some eternal and absolute right. But right and wrong are again meaningless apart from personality. The eternal right must be not mere right in the abstract, but a person who is essentially good and wills what is good.

Again, looking at humanity as a whole and at the course of human history, we cannot but recognize a common conscience, a sense that right is right, a craving for right against wrong, a belief that right is somehow the end and purpose of things. It is indeed most remarkable in this tragic and disordered scene of human life, where the majority of men seem to live and work more or less in defiance of right, or at least ignoring it, to note that they still pay this involuntary homage to right.

Moreover, it can hardly be denied that on an extended scale, if we look far enough and deep enough, this homage is justified. Right does tend ultimately to vindicate itself against wrong, and this triumph of right is accepted as the natural and right thing. Again, we are thrown back on the conclusion that the creator and Lord of the world is, in perfection, that goodness of which we see only blurred images on the stage of history. The fundamental cry of humanity is, 'Shall not the Judge of all the earth do right?' And where can

8   Can Men Know God ?

this demand come from, unless it is implanted in us by the Judge himself ?

So far, our conclusions have been derived simply from the consideration of the universe and of ourselves. They are at least cumulative proofs of the existence of God. Taken together they furnish very weighty presumption in favour of belief that he does exist ; so weighty that they throw the burden of disproof on those who deny it. To say that there is no God leaves unexplained the ancient and ineradicable tradition that there is. Moreover, it makes the universe and the human mind a puzzle to which there is no clue. If there is no mind in the universe answering to our own, no personal originator or guide of its order and law, no artist rejoicing in the infinite beauty and variety of his works, no righteous judge to whom conscience bears witness, then indeed we are faced by absolute contradictions. Man's highest faculties only deceive him. He is an exile in an incomprehensible and self-contradictory scheme of things.

WE reject the horrible alternative that this ordered universe is after all only chaos, and recognize that the weight of evidence is on the side of the believer in God's existence. We come now to grips with the problem which touches us most closely, our

Can Men Know God? 9

own personal relations with God. Is there any positive evidence that this God, whom reason acknowledges as the mind and soul and eternal rightness of the universe, can be personally known and communicated with? Has he spoken, does he speak to us? Can we speak to him?

Here it is evident that we can only draw our conclusions from human experience. There are no fiery messages written on the sky, which might compel men to believe. Men's thoughts about God, and the religious practices in which they have expressed them, have been extraordinarily varied and present a fascinating field of study. But in the history of religion there is one outstanding and unique fact. There is a collection of Hebrew writings which we commonly call the Old Testament, which claims to record a continuous series of personal divine dealings with men, and the existence from the beginning of history of 'a people of God' who were their recipients.

In this record there are many and varied strands of legend, history, legislation, ritual, poetry, philosophy, moral teaching. But there is a connecting thread of purpose. Just as the records of the rocks suggest inevitably some over-ruling guidance which brought nature's blind beginnings to the creation of man, so the Old Testament suggests a divine education of man's soul. God appears not only as the one personal eternal righteous being, but as one who is profoundly concerned with men, who leads the human race, through its chosen representatives, from infancy to manhood, making use of primitive, imperfect, even savage and erroneous ideas and customs, in order to guide men by slow degrees to higher conceptions both of God and of themselves.

The primitive belief in a tribal God passes into the nobler thought of a universal, omnipresent Lord of all men and of all the worlds. The narrow conception of a favoured and privileged nation is corrected by the revelation of Israel's vocation as the teacher of humanity. The fear of God as of one who will do harm unless he is propitiated gives place to the loftier teaching of the prophets that man can have God for his friend only by change of heart, by penitence, by purity, by just dealing, and by charity. The hope of a coming King, who will subjugate the heathen and place triumphant Israel on the throne of the world, is balanced and chastened by the picture of one who by his own suffering will bear the world's burden, and redeem mankind.

The teaching of those prophets who, from about the middle of the eighth century B.C., began to write their experiences, deserves close and special attention. They were not teachers of new doctrine: they inherited a long tradition. But the fact that they wrote and that their authentic writings have unquestionably been preserved, naturally gives a fixed and historical standing-point for estimating their importance.

Now these men are certain that God, who is the creator and universal Lord, the eternal righteousness, the guide and teacher of Israel in the past, has spoken to them. He has revealed himself to them as hating falsehood, injustice, and cruelty, as loving truth, purity, justice, charity, as the champion of right, whose purposes may be hindered but cannot be overcome by human sin, as the future redeemer and perfecter of humanity. And the impression which their writings produce on one who tries to read them with an open mind, is not only that the writers were sincere, but that their conviction was true. Their message is its own vindication. It is in harmony with all that we can surmise of God from contemplation of the universe and of ourselves. But it is more than that. It translates into human experience what could otherwise be no more than a hope or an aspiration, the fact that God not only exists, but that he takes the most living and intimate account of human life, that he desires to be known and served and loved, that he hears prayer and rewards effort and vindicates right.

This impression is further deepened by a study of the Psalms. A surface familiarity with these lyrics is apt to blind us to the really startling character of the experiences they record. What profound conviction they express of God's loving oversight and care, of his invincible righteousness, of his wrath against evil, of his majesty and his mercy, of his awful moral sovereignty, of his age-long guidance of men, of his tender sympathy with the poor, the suffering, the oppressed! It is a record of human experience which we simply cannot dismiss as an effort of fancy or devout imagination. The psalmists believed what they sang, they believed that they and others like them had had such actual experiences of God as justified their most glowing words. If there is nothing in all this, then indeed we are once more brought up against a blank wall of contradiction and despair.

Men have largely ceased to read the Bible, and they profess themselves no longer able to believe in a personal God. Let those who would fain recover faith begin again to read these books in their historical setting, with all the new light that comparative religion can throw on them; let them read them as if they were a new discovery; let them think out sincerely what they are, and what they imply, and they will probably find them absolutely startling and overwhelming.

Here is the finger of God, a flash of the will that can,
Existent behind all laws, that made them, and lo, they are.

Revelation of God in Jesus 13

WE claim then that in the Old Testament there is a line of direct evidence that God exists and desires to enter into fellowship with men. And this evidence reaches its climax in the appearance of Jesus Christ. The personality of Jesus, ever since he appeared, has arrested the attention of men. He has moved them to wonder, admiration, affection, to passionate loyalty, sometimes indeed to hatred and opposition, but he has seldom left them indifferent. Most men, even non-Christians, agree that his ethical teaching reached a height and a purity never equalled before or since, and that he himself was the highest expression of that teaching, the consummate flower of human character and worth.

The four gospels are worthy of a study and an attention which is scarcely ever given them by those who profess doubt about God's existence. Especially there are three out standing facts to be weighed.

(1) The whole of this phenomenal human life and teaching of Jesus was absolutely grounded on the conviction of God as the personal Father, Creator, Lover, Judge of men. God was to him the one supreme reality, the one object of human aspiration and obedience. From his first-recorded words in the Temple, 'Wist ye not that I must be in the things of my Father?' to his last dying words, 'Father, into thy hands I commend

14 Revelation of God in Jesus

my spirit,' and his message to the disciples after he was risen, 'I ascend unto my Father and your Father,' his whole career, the whole meaning of his life, is dominated by the belief in the Fatherhood of God.

(2) Jesus, throughout the gospels, the synoptists as well as St. John, identifies himself unmistakably with God as his 'Son,' as his authoritative interpreter, as the Lord of nature and human life, as the lawgiver and final judge of men. His followers, brought up though they had been in stern Jewish monotheism, accepted and worshipped him as such, and their belief has been passionately adhered to by the Christian Church in all ages, as the one justification of her claim to 'make disciples of all the nations.'

(3) Jesus represented himself as dying not merely as a martyr to truth, or to conquer death by his resurrection, but as a divine offering, inspired from the very heart of the Godhead, in order that he might reconcile God and man. Thus to the earlier revelation of God, whether drawn from contemplation of the universe and man, or from the Old Testament Scriptures, there is added the crowning fact of the divine love, a love so entire, so compassionate, that God wills even to sacrifice himself for the sake of his creatures.

If there be no God after all, or a God who is unknowable, the phenomenon of Jesus Christ and all the experience of Christians

Revelation of God in Jesus 15

stand simply without any possible explanation for rational beings. Is it thinkable that the highest human ideal, realized in a perfect character, an ideal and a character which are meaningless apart from God, were after all founded on a delusion ? Then, indeed, we can only accept the monstrous and self-contradictory conclusion of Mr. Bertrand Russell— 'only on the firm foundation of unyielding despair can the soul's habitation henceforth be safely built.'

Whatever be true, this cannot be. I dare not deny the best of which I am conscious in myself, reason, conscience, hope, love. Rather with humility and gratitude I take up again the foundation words of the Christian creed : ' I believe in God the Father almighty, maker of heaven and earth.' This belief sets me free, free from the appalling nightmare of a world without order and purpose. It harmonizes with what my reason recognizes as the reasonableness of the universe and my conscience testifies of the imperativeness of the moral law. It teaches me of a Father who is the first and the final cause of the universe, its creator and its artist, a Father whom I have learned to see and know for myself in the person of his Son Jesus, as the lover of men, who stoops in sympathy to me his creature, and who has for me his purpose and his calling, ' who loved me and gave himself for me.' In the light of this belief

16 Revelation of God in Jesus

alone can I find meaning and hope in human life, and in my own individual life.

That such a belief carries with it, in this present stage of being, many and great moral difficulties, such as the persistence of sin and pain, and the often unchecked arrogance of wrong—this I do not deny. But I know that I see such an infinitesimal part of the ways and works of the eternal God, that it seems to me but a right intellectual humility to leave these residual difficulties unsolved. I will not shut my eyes to the light, because it is sometimes mysteriously clouded. ' One thing I know, that whereas I was blind, now I see.'

THE CONGRESS BOOKS: No. 2

IS THERE A TRUE RELIGION?

A. E. J. RAWLINSON, **B.D.**
*Student & Tutor of Christ Church, Oxford,
Examining Chaplain to the Bishop of
Lichfield*

LONDON
THE SOCIETY OF
SS. PETER & PAUL
32 George St., Hanover Sq., W. 1, *and
The Abbey House, Westminster, S.W.* 1

Is there a True Religion ?

A CENTURY ago it was taken for granted in Europe and America, not indeed that the Christian religion was certainly true, but at least that all others were false. To-day this is no longer the case, and it is by no means uncommon to meet people who are quite doubtful about the truth of Christianity, but who yet are disposed to give a favourable hearing to the claims of some other religion, or (more commonly) to maintain that there is a truth behind all great religions which is more or less common to them all, and that the differences are not important.

It would be interesting to trace the reasons for this change which has undoubtedly taken place in people's minds. It is due, no doubt, in part to the widespread, if superficial, broadening of the popular outlook which has been one result of intercourse with non-European peoples, and of travel in non-European lands. In part it is due to the rise of such virtually new sciences as those of *cultural anthropology* (the study of the manners, beliefs, and customs of the various tribes and races of mankind) and

The Problem Stated 3

comparative religion (the study, in a scientific spirit, of the resemblances and differences between religions). No doubt we ought to allow something also for the influence of that general spirit of questioning which is so marked a characteristic of our time, and which is apt to create a prejudice in many persons' minds against the system of belief in which they happen to have been brought up—a prejudice which is sometimes combined with a quite uncritical acceptance of that which is foreign or unfamiliar to them.

The human soul is incurably religious, and yet at the same time the plain man is anxious not to be deceived. Aware that he is no expert in these matters, and yet aware also that there are other religious systems in the world besides that with which he is personally most familiar, he is apt to find himself reasoning somewhat as follows : ' Suppose I accept Christianity, will it be for any better reason than that which induces the Buddhist to accept Buddhism, namely, the fact that it is the religion of his fathers ? What am I really to think of all these competing religious systems and traditions ? May it not indeed be the case that there is in all of them equally some measure of spiritual truth ? Are they not all alike manifestations of the religious spirit of man ? Is there not in all human religion a genuine feeling after God, and is it not reasonable to suppose that, under whatever system of beliefs and practices and symbols, they that seek find?

'What advantage, then, has the Christian? Is there not, indeed, a kind of presumption in the claim made on behalf of any one particular revelation that it is higher than all the rest, that it (and it only) is the supreme and final truth? Why should the so-called " heathen " be " unchurched " ? Why cannot Christians be content to regard Christ and Krishna, Gautama and the Bâb, as being virtually equivalent manifestations, suited in different ways to the circumstances and attainments of different peoples, of one and the same divine principle manifested in different times and countries in slightly differing forms?'

Now, these are large questions, to which it is not easy to provide short answers within the compass of a tract. They raise the whole problem of the resemblances and differences between religions—of the differences, no less than of the resemblances. And it is obvious that when once this problem has thus been raised, the only really satisfactory way of dealing with it is actually to compare in detail the various religious systems with one another; to make a thorough study of them one by one; to ask, with regard to each of them, how it arose, how it developed and what changes (if any) it has passed through before reaching its present form; to try to assess the actual measure of truth and error which

Attitude to Heathen Faiths 5

each enshrines: and this involves a vast business, from which the plain man not unnaturally shrinks.

Moreover, the plain man cannot afford thus to wait for the problematical results of a lifetime of study. Consciously or subconsciously, he wants a faith he can live by, here and now. It would in fact be a poor result of a supposed enlargement of mind and outlook, if the discovery that there existed a number of different religious systems in the world, some of which present points of superficial resemblance to Christianity, were to be regarded as justifying or making necessary a half-acceptance and half-rejection of all alike, and an impartial refusal to practise the rites or accept the teaching of any particular one, whether Christian or other.

HAT can be done in a paper like this is not to provide a solution in detail of all these problems, but to suggest rather what the writer believes to be the true point of view from which they ought to be approached. We are apt to regard them as modern, and to forget that the Church has confronted them before. There was a 'conflict of religions' in the world into which Christianity came, which was at least as acute

6 Attitude to Heathen Faiths

as any conflict which confronts us to-day. The confusion of voices and the unsettlement of beliefs in modern Europe is not more radical than that which prevailed in the countries of the then civilized world around the Mediterranean when Christianity began.

It is not surprising, therefore, that the New Testament contains already hints and suggestions towards a Christian theory of Comparative Religion. The New Testament writings are in fact the documents, in the first instance, of a missionary Church: a Church which found itself confronted by the problem of how best to meet and deal with rival and competing religious systems, from the moment that it began to preach the gospel outside Palestine.

Speaking broadly, the account which the New Testament gives of the religions of heathenism is precisely the account which an enlightened Christian student of Comparative Religion might give of them to-day. At their worst, they are diabolical—' the things which the Gentiles sacrifice, they sacrifice to demons, and not to God ' (1 *Cor.* x. 20) ; they involve a degrading idolatry, in which men have ' changed the glory of the incorruptible God for the likeness of an image of corruptible man, and of birds, and four-footed beasts, and creeping things ' (*Rom.* i. 23) : they are corrupt and licentious—' God,' writes St. Paul, ' gave up ' the devotees of such heathen religions

Attitude to Heathen Faiths 7

'in the lusts of their hearts unto uncleanness, that their bodies should be dishonoured among themselves' (*Rom.* i. 24 ff.); nor will any one who has a real knowledge of the immoral cults and disgusting customs of the lower heathenism be disposed to regard St. Paul's language as being too strong.

On the other hand, considered on their higher side, the religions of heathenism are the expression in truth of a genuine seeking after the God who 'is not far from every one of us' (*Acts* xvii. 27); and to each and all of such genuine seekers after God, who indeed has not left himself 'without witness' (*Acts* xiv. 17), and to whom 'in every nation he that feareth him, and worketh righteousness, is acceptable' (*Acts* x. 35), the Church proclaimed, as she proclaims still, her triumphant gospel, 'whom therefore ye ignorantly worship, him declare I unto you' (*Acts* xvii. 23).

The attitude of Christianity towards heathen faiths can never in fact be anything else than this, for the reason that the very essence of Christianity, as a system of truth, is summed up in the affirmation that the revelation of God in Jesus Christ is the supreme and satisfying self-disclosure of God himself, the divine answer to the conscious or unconscious questionings and yearnings of the human spirit in its age-long search after the one true God. 'Oh, that I knew where I might find him, that I might come even to his seat'

8 No Compromise Possible

(*Job* xxiii. 3)—that is the age-long cry of the human soul; and to that cry Christianity makes answer 'The Son of Man came to seek and to save that which was lost' (*St. Luke* xix. 10).

NOW, this idea of the divine Arrival, the divine Advent or Coming, is the idea which is really important, characteristic, and central in Catholic Christianity: without it Christianity might indeed still claim (I think rightly) to be regarded as the highest among human religions, but would nevertheless have to be regarded as being in its nature like to other religions—an expression merely of the human ideal, of the search of man's soul after God. But Christianity is in fact the religion, not of man's search for God, but of God's search for man. The God of Christianity is compared to a shepherd, who seeks his lost sheep. In the gospel of Christianity the initiative is always with God.

The point has been illustrated by the example of a man seeking an interview with a great and important personage of whom he stands in awe. It is obvious that so long as it rests with him to take the initiative the whole burden of the interview is on his side. He does not in fact know in advance with what kind of reception he will meet: he screws up

No Compromise Possible 9

his courage, he rings the bell, he confronts the butler and mounts the stairs: but as he enters the great man's room and is at last in his presence his heart may well sink, and the very ticking of the clock make him afraid. People differ in nervousness, but the general picture is vivid enough: and it is an apt figure of the essential nature of human religion, so long as it is regarded simply as being the search of man's soul for God.

But how different it is if the great man comes himself and pays the call upon me, taking the trouble to mount my stairs and to seek me out, and giving an antecedent pledge and guarantee of his good will towards me by the very fact that he thus comes. The burden of the interview is in that case upon his side, no longer upon mine; and that is just the difference which the Incarnation makes: for it is this second picture which tallies with Christianity, the religion of the search of God for man.

If the Incarnation be true, there is in effect a true religion, compared with which all other religious faiths and systems are at best half-lights and partial hints and fore-shadowings of the truth, unconscious prophecies of a self-disclosure by God of himself which goes beyond them and completes and supersedes them. The religion of the Incarnation, supposing it to be true, would be of necessity the final and satisfying answer, the goal of man's long

10   Christianity Unique

spiritual pilgrimage and quest. For this reason it is clear that between Christianity and other religious faiths there can be no compromise, that the whole question turns around that of the truth or falsehood of the claims of Christianity itself. If it be true that Jesus Christ is indeed very God, manifested in terms of 'flesh' (that is, manhood) here among men, then clearly he at once fulfils and supersedes whatever is true in all heathen faiths, just as he at once fulfils and supersedes whatever was of temporary or partial value in Judaism itself.

CHRISTIANITY, of course, is not the only religion which has believed in an incarnation, or perhaps rather (a significant difference) in incarnations. Thus in the later developed or Mahayanist form of Buddhism[1] there is some kind of vague belief in God, and against this background a definite worship of the deified Buddha: a belief, indeed, in a whole series of Buddhas or 'enlightened ones,' each of whom is successively regarded

[1] In Mahayanist Buddhism there can be no question but that non-Buddhist influences have been at work. The original form of Buddhism as taught by Siddharta Gautama, 'the Buddha,' was an atheistic system (i.e., it involved no belief in God at all). Mahayanist Buddhism is found in China, Tibet, Mongolia, Corea, and Japan. The original Buddhism survives chiefly in Ceylon.

Christianity Unique 11

as having been a kind of incarnation of the heavenly Buddha. Or in that form of Hinduism which is known as Vaishnava Bhakti, devotion is paid to Vishnu, who is regarded as having been manifested in successive incarnations or 'avatars,' of whom Rama and Krishna are the most important. So too in what is known as Babi-Behaism, a religion derived from Mohammedanism in its Shiite form, there is belief in successive 'Imams' or partial incarnations of the uncreated light.

In all these cases there is, on historical grounds, a possibility—it does not really amount to much more—of Christian influence, direct or indirect, having been at work. A more significant point is the fact that 'the Buddhas and the Hindu avatars in the developed faiths are not historical personages,' while in Babi-Behaism 'the Imams were only partially conceived as actual incarnations at all.'[1] That to which the non-Christian types of incarnational religion bear witness is, in effect, rather the deep instinctive longing of the human soul for the manifestation of Deity in human nature, than the fact of any actual satisfaction of that longing. And with devotion to the abstract idea of divine incarnation, focussed merely upon a series of more or less legendary symbolic figures, neither the Christian Church nor the general heart of man can rest finally content.

[1] J. L. Johnston, *Some Alternatives to Jesus Christ*, p. 172.

12 Christianity Unique

The Christian gospel of the incarnate Christ is in fact unique : it is the one known case in which it has been asserted of a definitely historical person that he is to be worshipped as the incarnate Son of God, ' the same yesterday and to-day and for ever' (*Hebr.* xiii. 8). By the writer who has been already quoted, the distinguishing and characteristic marks of Christian devotion to Christ have been summed up as follows :

(*a*) As contrasted with other forms of religious belief in incarnation, Christianity has from the beginning maintained an unswerving insistence that the fundamental facts of the gospel story are historically true : the Church has insisted, that is to say, that the facts do matter, and that God, as a matter of historical fact, was incarnate in Jesus.[1]

(*b*) Christianity has maintained unswervingly the uncompromising claim that the revelation of God in Jesus Christ is unique and final. It has claimed to be the Catholic or universal religion, and has affirmed un-

---

[1] This, of course, does not preclude a critical study of the four gospels, or make it necessary to claim that every detail in the stories handed down to us must be in the strictest sense historically accurate. What it means is rather that if the gospel story as a whole could be shown to be mythical, or the facts to have been seriously distorted, our faith would be vain. As a matter of fact, it may fairly be claimed that historical criticism has refuted the 'Christ Myth' school of interpreters. On the present position of New Testament Criticism see my *Studies in Historical Christianity*, pp. 98-132.

The Christian God

waveringly that the Christ whom Christians adore is the one true Light of the World—all else can be but ' broken lights ' of him, shining with borrowed and reflected rays.

(c) Christians, while worshipping, have yet aspired to imitate their Saviour, in dependence upon the enabling power of the Holy Spirit ; wherefore true Christian worship has never been a mere passive dependence upon the incarnate Christ, a mere contemplation of him : Christianity, wherever it is genuine, drives men to some measure of definitely Christ-like action.

(d) Christianity appears to be unique in its doctrine of the Spirit, and the Christian Spirit is ever striving to refashion within the Church that which in Christ has been perfect once. And therefore, though Christianity looks back for its inspiration, it uses it in looking forward : its golden age is both past and future ; it looks back to the historic Incarnation, it looks forward to the future Advent, the final coming of the Christ, the kingdom of God.

NO other gospel can possibly claim to compare, in richness and fullness of spiritual meaning and spiritual power, with this gospel historically maintained by the Christian Church. And it is important to observe that it owes much of its strength to the doctrine of God, and of his relation to the world, which it inherited from the religion of the Jews. The God of Christianity is not a remote or unknowable Being, aloof from the world; nor again—as in the Pantheist form of philosophy which furnishes the background of Indian religions—is 'God' in Christianity just a name for the world as a whole, a mere Spirit of the All, present equally everywhere, so that all things are equally 'divine'; nor again (as some modern unorthodox teaching might seem to suggest) is God simply a personified name for the spiritual ideals of goodness and beauty and truth. He is alive, and he is active; distinct from the world, which depends upon him as its creator, and yet at work in the world as its sustainer; eternal, and yet having a purpose for the world and for men, which is wrought out in time.

On the Christian view God is the supreme agent in history, active and operative, and disclosing himself not simply through what he eternally is, but through what he continually does. Through the ages he works out his purpose, which man cannot fully understand, but to which the Church claims that Christ gives us a clue. For in the life and work of Jesus of Nazareth the Christian Church believes that she has witnessed a great act of God for man's salvation, the culmination of a great past and the beginning of a great future, and that the end is (as St. Paul puts it) ' to sum up ' eventually ' all things in Christ ' (*Ephes.* i. 10).

Such a view of the meaning of history I believe to be literally unique ; there is no other existing religion, not derived from, or influenced by, Judaism, which (so far as I know) has any view of the meaning of history at all. And it is only, I think, in the light of a faith which gives a meaning to history, and enables it to be read, not as a chapter of meaningless accidents or a perpetual recurrence of meaningless cycles, but as the slow working out of a purpose, and guided by God, that our life here in time can have meaning and dignity and value.

I would make one more claim for Christianity —the claim that its moral ideal is supreme. Here, again, it is not suggested that other religions are lacking in moral ideals. But it may fairly be said that Christianity is unique in the *degree* of its insistence upon the combination of religion and morals ; and unique also in combining an inexorable insistence on spiritual perfection as being the indispensable condition of the vision of God in its fullness, with the gospel of God's free forgiveness of sinners and the power of his Spirit to sanctify them wholly and to bring them at last to perfection. And it is matter of experience that where Christianity is genuinely practised, the ' fruits of the Spirit ' are indeed shown forth in lives that are genuinely Christ-like. Christianity is unique in its view of the character of God, as expressed in the character and life of his Son Jesus Christ: it is the character of absolutely holy and utterly self-sacrificing love, a character which combines sternness and strength with an infinite pity and compassion, with purity and tenderness and spiritual power to redeem. And the gospel proclaims that in his acquiring the character of sonship to God lies man's spiritual perfection; it invites men to accept in Christ Jesus the spiritual status of sons; and it undertakes by the power of the Spirit to make them anew. 'As many as received him, to them gave he power to become the sons of God, even to them that believe on his name—'Beloved, now are we the sons of God, and it doth not yet appear what we shall be: but we know that, when he shall appear, we shall be like him: for we shall see him as he is' (*St. John* i. 12; 1 *John* iii. 2).

Christianity, in the last resort, cannot, any more than any other ultimate philosophy of life or religious belief, be in the strict sense logically or theoretically 'proved.' But at least it cannot intelligibly be confused or combined with any other. It remains, whether true or false, the one intelligible hope of the world. And Christians have set their seal to it that it is true. 'This is the true God, and eternal life' (1 *John* v. 20).

THE CONGRESS BOOKS: No. 3

THE DOCTRINE OF THE TRINITY

PETER GREEN
Canon of Manchester,
Chaplain to the King

LONDON
THE SOCIETY OF
SS. PETER & PAUL
32 *George St., Hanover Sq., W.* 1, *and*
The Abbey House, Westminster, S.W. 1

The Doctrine of the Trinity

IN considering the doctrine of the blessed Trinity there are three things to be noted at the very beginning.

(i) First, the doctrine is not one which man could have found out for himself, by the exercise of his reason alone, apart from the revelation of God; nor, now that it has been revealed, can it be proved true by logical argument alone. It can be shown to be in agreement with reason, so that a philosopher, or man of science, can believe it without any disloyalty to truth, and without doing any violence to his intellect. But it cannot be proved by reason, so as to be obviously and necessarily true, quite apart from revelation.

Christians, so far from being ashamed of this fact, or unwilling to own it, should be proud of it, and should press it upon the attention of all with whom they discuss religious topics. If the Church had nothing to teach to her children which men could

4 Three First Considerations

not have found out for themselves, by the use of their own intelligence alone, Christianity would be a 'natural' religion, and not, as it is, a 'revealed' religion. But the Church has much to teach the world which man could never have found out for himself, though when it is shown to him he recognizes that it is true and helpful.

If we ask, 'How comes the Church with this special knowledge? What are the sources of her facts?' the answer is not difficult. She has two sources of such knowledge. One is, in the facts of the life of Jesus Christ, his Person and teaching. For 'no man . . . knoweth the Father, save the Son, and he to whomsoever the Son will reveal him' (*St. Matt.* xi. 27). The other is, in the constant guidance of God the Holy Spirit, helping her to understand those facts, and to make a right use of them. For our Lord promised that 'when he, the Spirit of truth, is come, he will guide you into all truth' (*St. John* xvi. 13).

A man may say 'I do not want, and will not accept this revealed religion; I will believe nothing that I cannot find out for myself by my own unaided intelligence.' But in every age, and in every country, the wisest and best of the heathen have always earnestly desired that God would reveal himself to man, and have even complained that he did not do so. Surely when the claim is made that God has, as a matter of fact, so revealed

Three First Considerations 5

himself to his children, the wise and truth-loving man will say, 'This is a claim that I must examine carefully, patiently, and reverently.'

(ii) Secondly, we must not expect the doctrine of the blessed Trinity to be simple and easy. We have a perfect right to ask that the Church shall state the doctrine as plainly as possible, so that every man may know what it is that the Church teaches, and what he himself is expected to believe. But we have no right to expect that the nature of God will prove an easy and simple thing to understand, to be grasped by any and every man without effort.

Some time ago a critic of religion wrote: 'For goodness' sake do not trouble me with theological puzzles. The religion I accept must be something quite simple and easy.' But what answer would be given to a boy who should walk into a night school and say to the teacher of chemistry, 'For goodness' sake do not trouble me with chemical formulae, and talk about atoms and molecular weights. The chemistry I accept must be quite simple and easy?' Would he not be told that there was no room for him in that night school, and that till he approached the subject in a humble and teachable spirit he had better stay away?

(iii) The last sentence suggests our third consideration. While it is certainly not true

6   How the Doctrine Arose

that all unbelievers are bad men—for there are many causes for an inability to believe, and many very good and noble men have been sceptics—it is equally certain that a bad, careless, vicious life is a very real and a very frequent cause of unbelief. For psychologists tell us that it is impossible to learn anything in which we have no interest. But a careless, indifferent, or vicious man cannot be really interested in God. So if we want to make progress in understanding religion we must strive to live it. That is to say, we must try to be good. For the text *St. John* vii. 17 should be translated, ' If any man sets his heart to do his will, he shall know the doctrine, whether it be of God.'

Keeping these three considerations in mind we may now go on to study the doctrine of the blessed Trinity. We must examine (i) the history of the doctrine, (ii) the meaning of the doctrine, and (iii) the arguments for its truth and value.

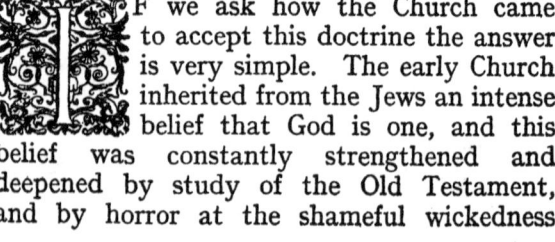

IF we ask how the Church came to accept this doctrine the answer is very simple. The early Church inherited from the Jews an intense belief that God is one, and this belief was constantly strengthened and deepened by study of the Old Testament, and by horror at the shameful wickedness

How the Doctrine Arose 7

and childish folly of the polytheistic heathen religions of the Roman Empire. It is impossible to read the early Fathers of the Church without recognizing the horror and contempt they show for the worship of the many and false gods of the heathen.

But at the same time Christians had the plain words of the New Testament to prove (*a*) that Jesus claimed a position, and an authority, which it would have been blasphemy for him to have claimed if he were not God; and (*b*) that the New Testament writers used language of Jesus Christ which they could not have used unless they had thought of Jesus as indeed 'over all, God blessed for evermore' (*Rom*. ix. 5). Let any candid man read the New Testament, stopping and asking himself from time to time, 'Could Jesus have spoken thus unless he claimed to be divine?' and 'Could the writer have used such words of Jesus unless he himself believed that Jesus was God?' and he will be forced to answer both questions in the negative. And the spiritual experience of the early Christians, as of all Christians in all ages, bore out and supported these claims. When they knew Jesus they knew him as God.

But exactly the same is true of God the Holy Ghost. The early Christians felt, as Christians have always felt and still feel, that the Holy Spirit who dwelt in them, teaching them, guiding them, and inspiring them

8   How the Doctrine Arose

to newness of life, was no vague influence or feeling, but a personal being, whom they could know, and between whom and their souls there could be real intercourse. And when they turned to the New Testament they found that it was as a 'Person' that Jesus had spoken of the Holy Spirit, describing his active working as guide, teacher, and inspirer of the Church. And all writers of the New Testament use similar language.

So the early Church was forced to believe the two facts, that God is one, and that the Father is God, the Son God, and the Holy Ghost God. But this is precisely the doctrine of the blessed Trinity. It is firmly based on the teaching of holy Scripture and on the witness of Christian experience in all ages. The Church must hold both sides of the doctrine. In loyalty to holy Scripture and in loyalty to her own spiritual experience she dare not give up either side of the truth. Both statements must be true, both must be taught and believed.

Down to the time of the great Council of Nicaea in A.D. 325 the Church was struggling to find suitable language in which to express her faith in the unity of the Godhead and the reality and distinctness of the Persons. Sometimes, in laying stress on the unity, some Christian writers seemed in danger of forgetting the distinctions of Person. Sometimes, in emphasizing the reality of Christ's divinity,

How the Doctrine Arose 9

or the personality of the Holy Ghost, some of them seemed to be in danger of falling into tritheism, the heresy, that is to say, of teaching belief in three Gods. But always the guidance of the Holy Spirit kept the Church in the right path, and helped her to choose the right words and phrases in which to express her faith.

Indeed, it is impossible to read the history of the first four or five centuries of Christianity without an ever-deepening sense of how God has guided his Church. Again and again it would have been so easy—one might almost say so natural—to have accepted the wrong expression. Yet now, looking back over the centuries, we can see how the seemingly harmless expressions which the Church refused to accept would have robbed the faith of all power and life, whereas the expressions she was guided to accept were perfectly fitted to preserve 'the faith . . . once delivered to the saints' (*Jude* 3).

Critics of Christianity sometimes speak as if the long struggles of the early Church to win a scientific expression of her faith (for that is what theology is, a scientific statement of the facts of religious experience) were a proof that the doctrine of the blessed Trinity was not part of the faith of the primitive Church. It would be just as sensible to say that the solar system had no existence till Copernicus, Kepler, and Newton taught men

The Nature of God

how to explain the movements of the sun, moon, and planets. The movements of the heavenly bodies were the facts for which men of science had to find a coherent expression. The unity of God, the deity of Jesus Christ, and the personality of the Holy Spirit, are the facts for which the great theologians of the early Church had to find a coherent expression. They accepted, and we accept, the doctrine of the blessed Trinity because it is a full, perfect, and adequate expression of the facts. It adds nothing to the faith set forth in the New Testament; and if St. Paul and St. John and St. Peter came back to earth to-day we may be sure they would say of our creeds, ' Yes, those words express very clearly and simply what we believed and taught.'

WHAT then exactly does the doctrine mean? Men often say, ' How can three Persons be one God?' Let us suppose that there were a being, some kind of angel, or visitor from the planet Mars, who had never seen anything alive. How difficult he would find it to understand the fact of growth. He would easily understand how a thing can increase, so to speak, from outside, as a pile of stones becomes larger and larger as more stones are thrown on to it. But he would find it

The Nature of God

hard to understand how anything could grow, so to speak, from inside, and by itself. The idea of growth would be to him a thing very hard to grasp. And if he were conceited, impatient, and unteachable, he would almost certainly fail altogether to understand it.

Now let us suppose that this same strange being, having learned something about life and growth, as displayed in trees and plants, were introduced to a new fact, namely, that of intelligence, as displayed in the higher animals. How difficult he would find it to understand what is meant by liking and disliking, choosing and refusing, knowing or being ignorant. If life is hard to understand, how much more difficult is mind. Here, too, he would need to be humble, patient, and teachable if he were to grasp these ideas. But as soon as he began to understand what is meant by mind and how it works, he would have to try to understand something higher than mind, as we find it in animals; he would have to consider personality, as found in human beings. Here again he would be confronted by something new, strange, and not to be explained by reference to anything with which he had hitherto met. He would have to be careful, humble, and teachable.

Yet two things he ought to have learned by now, namely, that existence is known to us at various levels, as matter, life, consciousness, personality; and that many of the mis-

The Nature of God

takes in men's thinking are due to the effort to explain the higher by the lower.[1]

He then, our angel or visitor from Mars, will expect, and we too shall do well to expect, that when we pass from considering the nature of man to considering the nature of God we shall find something new. We can contrast the nature of man and the nature of God as follows:

The Nature of Man. The human race, as we know it by experience, consists of an infinite number of minds or persons, each of which is separated from all other minds, and shut up within the circle of its own identity so that one mind cannot ordinarily share the thoughts, feelings, and desires of other minds except by means of the medium of speech.[2] And secondly, in each mind or person only a part of human nature is displayed, so that ' it takes all sorts to make a world.'

The Nature of God. The Godhead, as we

---

[1] For instance, in the discussions about Free Will, which were in fashion five and twenty years ago, it was the habit of unbelievers to compare a man with a gun, or a watch, or a pair of boots. All such comparisons were absurd. You cannot adequately compare a mind with a thing.

[2] This isolation and loneliness of each mind or person is a frequent topic among poets. The reader should read Matthew Arnold's *Isolation* (*Poems of M. Arnold*, World's Classics, p. 121), or Lord Houghton's *Strangers Yet* (*Golden Treasury of Songs and Lyrics*, Second Series, p. 88), or Francis Thompson's *A Fallen Yew* (*Selected Poems*, p. 48). But the idea is common to many poets and thinkers.

The Nature of God

know it by revelation, consists of three minds or Persons, each of whom is perfectly one with the others, sharing every act of knowledge, love, and will, so that there is no barrier of individuality between the Persons. And secondly, in each person the entire nature of God is displayed, so that 'we are compelled by the Christian verity to acknowledge every person by himself to be God and Lord' (*Athanasian Creed*).

We can get a faint picture of this life of God in the following way. Every one must have noticed how, when a man and a woman have lived together in perfect love for many years they seem hardly to need to speak. They have become so closely united in thought and will and desire that the barrier between the one soul and the other seems to have been broken down. If we imagine that love heightened a million times, so that the oneness, the unity, likewise is deepened a millionfold, we get some faint picture of the perfect unity of the three Persons in the blessed Trinity.

Does not the doctrine of the blessed Trinity, as here stated, go dangerously near to tritheism, or a belief in three Gods? No, for we do not believe in three Persons all of whom are independent and self-existing. That has never been the doctrine of the Church. The Father alone is self-existing; that is to say, he alone exists through his own power. The other two Persons are derived and draw their

14 Philosophical Analogies

life from the Father. 'The Father hath life in himself;' he has 'given to the Son to have life in himself' (*St. John* v. 26). And we say of the Holy Spirit that he 'proceedeth (that is, draws his life from) the Father and the Son' (*Nicene Creed*: compare *St. John* xv. 26, xvi. 7).

Here again, if we are careful to remember that comparisons and analogies are poor and weak in such cases, we may think of God the Father as an eternally burning light, and of God the Son as the reflection of that light in a mirror (compare *Hebr.* i. 3), and of the Holy Spirit as the radiance streaming out from the light and from its reflection in the mirror. But such an analogy must not make us forget that we believe in three divine Persons, not in one Person acting in three different ways. For that is not the Christian faith revealed by God.

THE strongest argument for the truth of the doctrine of the blessed Trinity is that it alone is adequate to meet the facts of holy Scripture and religious experience. After centuries of discussion no other forms of words could be found which would give expression to all sides of the truth.

But there are many things which confirm

our faith in it. This doctrine which was accepted, not in obedience to the teaching of philosophers, but as it were in their very teeth, and was indeed 'hid from the wise and prudent and . . . revealed unto babes' (*St. Matt.* xi. 25), has, in the centuries that have passed since the Council of Nicaea, received wonderful support. Many different lines of human experience and human thinking lead up to, and find their fulfilment and explanation in, this doctrine. We can only notice one or two ; thus—

(i) *Mysticism.* All the great mystics, especially the most original and independent, as Plotinus the Greek mystic, Eckhart and Boehme the Germans, and some of the Sufi (Mohammedan) and Buddhist mystics, who have claimed first hand experience of the nature of God, have taught a doctrine of spirit which strangely supports the Christian doctrine of the blessed Trinity.

(ii) *Philosophy.* The result of twenty-five centuries of philosophy might almost be summed up by saying, that a philosopher can neither give up belief in separate and immortal souls (that is, in the doctrine of personality) nor retain a belief in distinct individuals wholly separate from each other without falling into confusion and contradiction. If, remembering that man was created in the image of God, he accepts the Church's doctrine of the blessed Trinity as his guide

Philosophical Analogies

to the true nature of man, he gains clear guidance at once.

(iii) In *Ethics*, the science of right and wrong, and in *Sociology*, the science of society, the idea of a community life, in which the life of mere individuality is absorbed into, but not lost in, a higher unity, becomes daily of greater importance.

(iv) *Mathematicians*, in studying the idea of infinity, quite apart from the idea of an infinite God, have been led to a doctrine of the infinite which strangely reflects the Church's doctrine of the blessed Trinity.

There are many other lines of thought we might pursue, but space forbids. It is enough that if any foolish, ignorant, or wicked person makes a mock of this deep mystery we can only reply that it alone reconciles and justifies all the facts of holy Scripture and Christian experience, and that it is also the most precious gift of God the Holy Ghost to the intellectual life of man, shedding light as it does on many of the most difficult problems of philosophy.

THE CONGRESS BOOKS: No. 4

THE DEITY OF CHRIST

N. P. WILLIAMS, B.D.
Fellow of Exeter College, Oxford,
Examining Chaplain to the Bishop
of Newcastle

LONDON
THE SOCIETY OF
SS. PETER & PAUL
32 *George St., Hanover Sq., W.* 1, *and*
The Abbey House, Westminster, S.W. 1

The Deity of Christ

IT is always as well, for the sake of clearness, to state at the beginning of a brief essay to whom its contentions are meant to appeal, and what will be taken for granted in it. This essay is addressed to a man whom I met some sixteen years ago in the train between Newcastle and York. I have never seen him since, have no idea of his name, and do not know whether he is alive or dead; but I take him as typical of the 'man in the street,' who is generally interested, or at any rate prepared to be interested, in religious questions, but does not feel sufficiently convinced of the truth of any one doctrinal system to be able to attach himself to any sect or denomination

I remember well how this, my unknown friend, informed me that he believed firmly in a good and omnipotent God, in the power of prayer, and in the obligatory character of what would generally be accepted as Christian morality; but that, whilst venerating the historic Christ as one of the greatest and best of mankind, he had never seen any convincing reason for attributing to him a transcendental or super-

4 Christ and the Roman World

human being, or any sort of identity with the supreme Godhead; and that, consequently, the doctrine of the Trinity (which is almost inevitably necessitated by the inclusion of Christ within the sphere of Absolute Deity, coupled with the preservation of the distinction between him and the Father to whom he prayed) appeared to him as so much metaphysical nonsense.

The following considerations are addressed to this man and to any others like him into whose hands this tract may come. They are meant to suggest that, given the premisses which he accepted, namely, the existence of God, the historicity of Jesus Christ, and the permanent validity of Christian morals, no other explanation of the personality of Christ is really satisfactory, either to head or heart, than that which is the core of historic Christianity, and is summed up in the majestic phrases, 'God of God, Light of Light, Very God of Very God, Begotten not made, Being of one substance with the Father, By whom all things were made.'

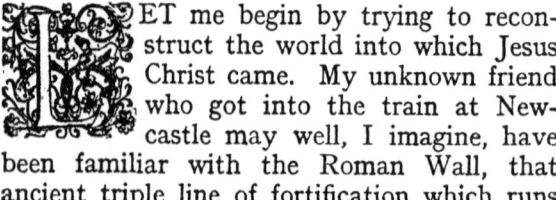ET me begin by trying to reconstruct the world into which Jesus Christ came. My unknown friend who got into the train at Newcastle may well, I imagine, have been familiar with the Roman Wall, that ancient triple line of fortification which runs

Christ and the Roman World 5

from the Solway Firth to Wallsend on the Tyne; which, with its battlements, mound, and ditch, was the 'Hindenburg Line' of those days, protecting the fertile and civilized province of Roman Britain from the incursion of the barbarous Picts and Scots who lived to the north of it. We can still trace the outlines of the fortresses which studded its length at intervals; we can wander through the commanding officers' quarters, investigate the cellars which contained the apparatus for heating their baths, and note the deep ruts worn in the stone thresholds of the gates by the iron-clad wheels of the heavy Roman war-chariots, the 'tanks' of that day.

It is true that the Roman Wall was built a century after the death of Jesus Christ; but I speak of it now because it is a thing of which every Englishman has heard, and brings home to us, as nothing else perhaps can, the might and majesty of that great Roman power which dominated the known world at the beginning of our era. It was a vast Empire including the countries which we now know as England, France, Spain, the Rhineland, Switzerland, Italy, Austria proper, Yugo-Slavia, Greece, Asia Minor, Armenia, Syria, Egypt, Tripoli, Algeria, Tunis, and Morocco, enclosing the Mediterranean in its bosom as an exclusively Roman lake. In theory, all these countries were governed by the Republican City-State of Rome, but in actual fact by the Emperor

6 Christ and the Roman World

Augustus, whose power, though carefully camouflaged under Republican forms, was that of a military monarch, resting upon a standing army of a hundred and fifty thousand men.

If we leave out of account the remote and fossilized empire of China, the Roman State was the only world-power which then existed upon this planet; it was, at that date, the supreme political achievement of mankind, an achievement so great that it seemed, even to those who had brought it into being, to be supernatural in character; it possessed an elaborate material civilization, including restaurants, banks, joint-stock companies, fire brigades, a postal service, and what we now call 'Turkish baths,' a civilization on which no serious advance was made until the discovery of gun-powder and printing, fourteen centuries later; it possessed the accumulated thought and literature of Greece, upon which little improvement has been made even down to the present day, and the treasures of its art, upon which no improvement has ever been made.

It was within the shelter of this great and splendid fabric that Jesus Christ was born, lived, and died. If we can imagine a Roman man of letters, let us say Seneca, being sufficiently interested in him to put down on paper a brief account of his life, it would run somewhat as follows: 'On the eastern frontier of the Empire there is a small, third-class

Christ and the Roman World 7

province called Judaea. This is the original home of an unpleasant and barbarous nation known as the Jews, who have colonies in most of our great cities, and are generally detested for their turbulence, usuriousness, and unsociability. In this backwater of civilization there recently appeared a young artisan of obscure parentage, who caused a certain amount of excitement amongst his barbarous compatriots by claiming to be a kind of Mahdi, or "Messiah" as they call it, and by denouncing the superstitions and vices of the priests and the pious members of his nation.

'At first it looked as though his movement might have some little success, and might be a nuisance to our local administration and garrisons. Fortunately, however, the conspicuous lack of tact with which this agitator pursued his mission, and his curious unwillingness to identify himself with anything like an armed revolt, had the effect of alienating the sympathies of the extreme nationalist party, who, in order to get rid of him, denounced him for high treason to our local governor, Pontius Pilatus. Pilatus, though his abilities would never have qualified him for more than a third-rate governorship on the frontier of the Empire, dealt with the matter quite competently; he had the agitator executed, with the result that his adherents dispersed, and the whole movement, which at one time

8 What Happened Later

looked as if it might be rather troublesome, happily came to an end.

'The doings of this person, whose whole public career (if it can be dignified by that name) only lasted for two years, and who never succeeded in emerging from the obscurity of one of the least-known of our provinces, are only of interest to the historian, and have, it need hardly be said, produced not the slightest effect upon the fabric of Roman culture, religion, and thought. It is much to be wished that all provincial governors would display the same tact and good sense as Pontius Pilatus in utilizing the religious passions of these barbarous tribes in order to get rid of inconvenient agitators, and the same promptness in suppressing fanatical movements at their outset, before they attain to proportions which may involve the Imperial Government in the trouble and expense of a punitive expedition.'

SUPPOSE now, for the sake of argument, that I am able to mount a time machine like that imagined by Mr. H. G. Wells, to travel back into the first century A.D., taking with me all my accumulated knowledge of the centuries which have elapsed since that date, and to pay a call upon Seneca

What Happened Later 9

in his pleasant country house at Nomentum. Having explained that, for various reasons, I happen to possess an absolutely accurate and certain knowledge of the course of history subsequent to his day, I proceed as follows:
'You remember that obscure Syrian artisan about whom you wrote a brief paragraph the other day; and probably you remember dismissing the subject with the remark that his life and death were of no permanent importance whatsoever. That dictum was, no doubt, justifiable, on the basis of the knowledge which you then possessed. But, on the basis of my knowledge, I am able to tell you some facts which will probably surprise you a good deal.

'Shortly after his death, his followers re-assembled, saying that they had seen him, risen from the dead, that they had conversed with him, and even shared meals with him (*Acts* x. 41). On the basis of this alleged resurrection of their Master, and of the Messianic claims which he made, they are proclaiming him as a divine being. They are preaching a new Oriental religion, not unlike those with which you are already familiar, the Phrygian, Syrian, or Egyptian Mysteries, only with the figure of Jesus of Nazareth set in its centre as the divine Redeemer, the Saviour-God, instead of Attis or Osiris. They are now hard at work propagating this new cult in Asia Minor and Greece, with the most passionate enthusiasm and the most

What Happened Later

unflinching resolution; and their advance missionaries have even got as far as Rome itself.'

At this point we may imagine Seneca as interjecting: 'So far, what you have told me does not surprise, though it grieves me: I know the folly of human nature too well to be surprised at the popularity of any fantastic cult coming from the East, even the cult of an executed criminal; and I only wish that the Senate had made a firm stand against these foreign superstitions at the very beginning of their invasion of the West, in the days of the Second Punic War.'

'However,' I go on, 'I am afraid that what I am now going to say will be a real shock to you. This Judaean cult, instead of dying out after a time, will continue to gather strength and solidity until it finally attracts the attention of the Imperial Government. The Caesars and their advisers will make periodical efforts during the next three centuries to stamp it out altogether, by presenting its adherents with the choice between abjuration and death.'

'Quite right too,' interjects Seneca.

'In spite, however, of the most determined efforts of several Emperors, backed up by all the resources of the Roman State and the practical unanimity of public opinion, to suppress this new religion, it will, in a most unaccountable manner, gain ever more and

What Happened Later 11

more adherents. For every one person who is thrown to the beasts, ten will join the new society; and, finally, just about 250 years from now, the Roman government will confess itself beaten, the religion of Jesus will be given full liberty to exist, and an Emperor will ascend the throne who will profess himself a believer in the deity of the Nazarene. From that moment onward the triumph of the new religion will be secured: the traditional gods of Rome will gradually be forgotten, and the new cult will become the State religion of the Empire.

'Then the Empire will be broken to pieces by the savage races from beyond the Alps, who will set up new barbarous kingdoms upon its ruins; Rome will be laid waste, and her shrunken population will not fill a third of the space within her ancient walls. But the religion of Christ will survive, and subdue the rude barbarians under its yoke, until Christianity and civilization have become synonymous: and, nineteen centuries hence, when the very name of Caesar has passed away, and the achievements of Rome are known only to scholars and learned men—when the mechanical arts have developed to such an unheard-of extent that men can hear each other's voices speaking through the ether in places hundreds of miles apart, and are able to travel in three hours through the air from Londinium to Colonia Agrippinensis in great

12 What Happened Later

winged ships—the religion of Jesus will have conquered not merely Europe, but even greater continents now unknown, lying beyond the western seas. The ill-omened gibbet on which he died will have become the golden symbol of self-sacrifice and love, blazing on the diadems of kings, the domes of temples, and the breasts of heroes; and the first day in every seven, the day following the Jewish Sabbath, will be observed, in memory of his resurrection, throughout the civilized world. Nineteen centuries hence, the real and nominal adherents of his worship will together make up one-third—and that the most highly-cultivated one-third—of the human race.'

What would be Seneca's reply? It would be, undoubtedly, somewhat as follows: 'What you are saying is nothing but delirious raving. It is flatly contrary to the reason, nature, and necessity of things. If a thing so crazy as the cult of an executed carpenter can really conquer the power of Rome, then anything may be true, and anything may happen. If I could believe that this Galilean superstition will win such an overwhelming triumph in the teeth of reason, common sense, tradition, decency, and patriotism, I should have to believe that the carpenter really was divine, and I cannot frame any more preposterous supposition than that. You are obviously demented.'

Christ at least a Superman

I HAVE indulged in this flight of imagination in order to bring home to my readers the fact that the existence, the wide diffusion, and the prodigious vitality of Christianity at the present day, are, in themselves, the most astonishing facts in history. The average man has probably never reflected very deeply upon the origins of Christianity, and is inclined, in a vague, general way, to take its existence for granted, as a perfectly normal and natural fact: but if he will consider the argument of the foregoing paragraphs carefully and fairly, he will, I think, admit that the plain undeniable facts of history prove at least this, beyond the shadow of a doubt—that Jesus Christ was by far the greatest, most powerful, and most astonishing personality that has ever appeared on the surface of this planet: that he was, at the very least, what modern writers call a 'Superman.'

We all admire the energy and the greatness of a man who, with no powerful friends and no advantages, raises himself, by sheer force of personality, from humble circumstances to the foremost position in the State:

Who breaks his birth's invidious bar,
　And grasps the skirts of happy chance,
　And breasts the blows of circumstance,
And grapples with his evil star;

14 Christ God's Messenger

> Who makes by force his merit known,
> And lives to clutch the golden keys,
> To mould a mighty State's decrees,
> And shape the whisper of the throne.

But, bearing this in mind, what must we say of a man, also possessing no advantages of birth, family, friends, or education, who, in two years of what was on the whole unpopular activity, spent in one of the backwaters of civilization and ending in a criminal's death, succeeded in stamping the impress of his personality so deeply upon human history that during nineteen succeeding centuries millions of the human race, including its best and wisest, have worshipped him with rapturous adoration as almighty God in person? If my friend in the train will think calmly and quietly over these facts, he will, I think, be prepared to admit at least this—that Jesus Christ stands in a category entirely by himself, as the Superman, the central figure of history, the supreme instance of the power of personality.

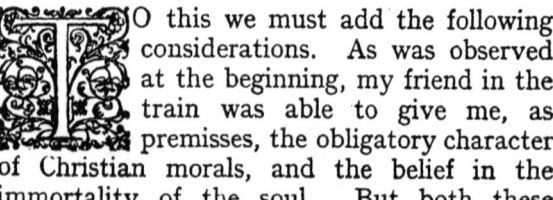TO this we must add the following considerations. As was observed at the beginning, my friend in the train was able to give me, as premises, the obligatory character of Christian morals, and the belief in the immortality of the soul. But both these

Christ God's Messenger

things are admittedly the gifts of Jesus himself to the world. Even the most refined and enlightened public opinion in the ancient world saw no grave harm in infanticide, in the crucifixion of slaves by their masters for trifling reasons, and in modes of conduct which all right-minded men would now describe as dark and hideous vices; and before Christ, the hope of immortality, which for the majority of spiritually-minded men is the one thing which makes life worth living, existed in the world only in the dimmest and vaguest form. The early Christian writer is entirely in the right, as a matter of mere indisputable historic fact, when he says that it was Christ who ' brought life and immortality to light through the gospel ' (2 *Tim.* i. 10).

However—if my friend in the train is sincere, as I do not doubt him to be, when he tells me that he accepts the validity of the Christian ethic—it will be sufficient on this point for me to quote the well-known words of John Stuart Mill, which have a peculiar impressiveness as coming from an avowed agnostic :

' About the life and sayings of Jesus there is a stamp of personal originality combined with profundity of insight, which, if we abandon the idle expectation of finding scientific precision where something very different was aimed at, must place the Prophet of

16 Christ God's Messenger

Nazareth, even in the estimation of those who have no belief in his inspiration, in the very first rank of the men of sublime genius of whom our species can boast. When this pre-eminent genius is combined with the qualities of probably the greatest moral reformer, and martyr to that mission, who ever existed upon earth, religion cannot be said to have made a bad choice in pitching upon this man as the ideal representative and guide of humanity; nor, even now, would it be easy, even for an unbeliever, to find a better translation of the rule of virtue from the abstract into the concrete, than to endeavour so to live that Christ would approve our life' (*Three Essays on Religion*, 1874, p. 254).

If we put these two conclusions together, which simply follow from the facts of history, when coupled with the premisses which my friend in the train has already given me—the conclusions, namely, that Jesus was the greatest and most spiritually powerful man who has ever appeared on earth, and that he was the greatest moral and spiritual benefactor of the human race—it follows that he may, and should, be described as being, at the very least, the supreme Messenger of God to humanity, the supreme representative of the Most High in the sphere of human history.

Is He also God?

I SHOULD like, at this stage, to point out that what I have said so far has been based solely upon historical facts which no one can deny, and upon the assumptions which my friend in the train has been willing to give me; I have made no appeal to the authority of the creeds, or of the Church, because I am arguing with a man who tells me that he does not accept this authority. But I venture to hope that, so far, I have brought my friend with me.

I imagine that, at this point, his thoughts would run somewhat as follows: 'Well, I am willing to admit that what you have just said appears to be cogent, and I am prepared to revise and heighten my estimate of the person of Jesus Christ correspondingly. In the light of the considerations which you have brought forward, and which I am bound to say that I had not previously realized, I think I am now ready to regard him, not merely as 'a very great and good man,' but also as 'the supreme Man of all time'; and, if there is a solution of the perplexities and troubles of weary, war-scarred humanity, I daresay that he possesses the secret of it.

'But there is still a considerable gulf between this and the Christology of the Catholic Church. Even a Superman, if he is no more than that, is only a creature, and must, therefore, be separated by an infinite abysm from the most high Creator himself. I am not yet convinced that the facts to which you have pointed require a real incarnation of God himself, or that they are beyond the reach of perfect manhood, inspired by divine influences: and I am too honest to claim the privileges of the Church's life on the basis of a mere vague affirmation of " divinity " as distinct from " deity "; nor, I imagine, is that what you want me to do. You have shown me that Christ is an enigma, the central enigma of history; and that his life and death are very far from being the simple and straightforward facts which I had unreflectingly thought them to be; but you have not yet convinced me that the ascription of deity to him is the true solution.'

NOW, if my friend in the train will again reflect for a moment, he will, I think, admit that the solution of the enigma, if there is one, must presumably be that propounded by Christ himself. If he is the supreme Messenger of God, that part of his message which relates to himself must be taken as true. It is very difficult indeed, if not impossible, to conceive of the supreme Messenger of God as being in the right on all other points, but in the wrong on the question of his own nature: a divine Messenger who

Christ's own Claims 19

had failed to comply with the Greek adage γνῶθι σεαυτόν, 'know thyself,' would be almost a contradiction in terms. The line of thought which we have pursued so far must, then, predispose us to believe in any explanation which we can find in the authentic sayings of Christ with regard to his own nature and his relations to the God who sent him. We will, therefore (following our method of building upon nothing which is not reasonably certain and admitted by all persons of education and intelligence), turn to the fundamental documents which contain the primary accounts of Jesus' life and teaching—that is, to the gospels.

The assured results of modern research in regard to these ancient biographies of Jesus Christ will be found summarized in another pamphlet in this series, and my own statement on the question of their literary authority must, therefore, be of the briefest. In what follows I do not propose to make any use of the Gospel according to St. John (although I personally believe it to be a reliable historical document), because its authority in this sense is not universally admitted. In accordance with the general principle of building the structure of our argument only upon what is absolutely unchallenged by reasonable and educated persons, we will confine ourselves to the Synoptic Gospels, that is, the first three.

With regard to these, scholars are fairly

well agreed that behind them lie two even more ancient documents: (1) an edition compiled by John Mark of St. Peter's reminiscences of the life and sayings of Christ, which is, for all practical purposes, identical with our present Gospel of St. Mark; and (2) a document known by the symbol 'Q' (the first letter of the German word *Quelle*, 'source'), containing a collection of our Lord's sayings as transmitted to the compiler by actual hearers. Generally speaking, the consensus of critical opinion holds that from 'Q' are drawn those sayings of Christ which are recorded in common by St. Matthew and St. Luke, but not by St. Mark. These primitive records (which may safely be dated as at any rate not later than about A.D. 70 and A.D. 60 respectively) thus contain what is for all practical purposes first-hand testimony, and provide far better evidence for the life of Christ than that which we possess of the lives and sayings of many of the great characters of antiquity. To them, therefore, let us go.

As we interrogate these documents the following conclusions emerge with unmistakable clearness. Jesus asserted an authority far transcending that claimed by any of the prophets of the Old Testament. He claimed the right to cancel, by a mere *ipse dixit*, a

Christ's own Claims 21

permission believed to have been given by Moses with Jehovah's direct authority (*St. Mark* x. 4). He claimed to exercise the divine prerogative of forgiving sins (*St. Mark* ii. 5). He led his disciples to expect a Messianic kingdom, in which he would be king, and in which he would make them princes (*St. Matt.* xix. 28; *St. Luke* xxii. 29). He asserted that he would be the Judge of quick and dead at the last great day of God (*St. Mark* viii. 38; *St. Matt.* vii. 23; *St. Luke* xiii. 27). He claimed to be the Son of God in a sense which, whilst undefined, was absolutely unique and distinctive (*St. Mark* xii. 6; xiii. 32). He sometimes describes God as 'your Father,' sometimes as 'my Father,' but he never brackets himself with his disciples in describing God as 'our Father.'[1] The highest point to which this unique claim rises in the mouth of Jesus is contained in the wonderful saying found in *St. Matt.* xi. 25–27; *St. Luke* x. 21, 22, a saying undoubtedly derived from ' Q ' and indisputably an utterance of Jesus, spoken in a moment of supreme ecstasy : ' . . . All things have been delivered unto me of my Father : and no one knoweth the Son, save the Father ; neither doth any

---

[1] The single apparent exception to this, in the Lord's Prayer as given by St. Matthew, is not strictly accurate ; the earliest and best text, as given by St. Luke, begins with the single word 'Father': and in any case the prayer was intended to be used by the disciples, not by Christ himself.

know the Father, save the Son, and he to whomsoever the Son willeth to reveal him.'

Here Jesus definitely brackets himself together with God as an almost co-ordinate power; and by asserting that his own nature is such that only the infinite God can comprehend it, he implicitly ascribes infinity to himself. After this, it is not surprising to find that he claims a limitless personal devotion, which is to stop at nothing (*St. Matt.* x. 37; *St. Luke* xiv. 26); that he asserts that in some mysterious sense his death will be a ransom for many (*St. Mark* x. 45), and his blood will consecrate the new covenant between God and man (*St. Mark* xiv. 24); and that to the High Priest's crucial question ' Art thou the Messiah, the Son of the Blessed One?' he replies with the tremendous affirmation, ' I am; and ye shall see the Son of Man sitting at the right hand of power, and coming with the clouds of heaven' (*St. Mark* xiv. 61, 62).

NOW, all these facts, taken together, cannot be fairly interpreted as less than a claim to be a super-human person, the Son of God in a lofty, unique, and mysterious sense, possessing a filial relation to the Most High not shared by any form of created being; a claim which, if accepted by his followers, as it was, would necessarily lead them to worship him.

'Either God or Mad'

And, when we remember that we have gathered this claim, not from the works of St. Paul or St. John or any subsequent interpreter of the life of Christ, nor yet from the parts of St. Matthew's and St. Luke's gospels which are peculiar to those writers, but from his own most indisputably authentic sayings and doings, as contained in the bed-rock documents, Mark and 'Q,' which represent the testimony of first-hand witnesses, we shall see that we have come to a point at which it is impossible to evade the question—Was this claim true, or was it not?

If our previous conclusions have been true, namely, that Christ was the supreme Messenger of God to humanity, this claim also must be true. There is an old saying, *Aut deus aut non bonus*: 'Either he was God or he was not a good man.' In other words, if Christ's claims were not true, then they must be regarded as the last word in intolerable arrogance. Perhaps, nowadays, we should phrase it, *Aut deus aut vesanus*: 'Either he was God, or he was beside himself.' (And the latter estimate, we may remember, was formed about him by his opponents during his lifetime.) I do not see how it is possible to evade the horns of this dilemma. If he was not the Son of God in this exalted, transcendent sense, he must have been suffering from that distressing form of mental disease, of which instances are found in every asylum

24 Theological Formulation

to-day, in which the patient imagines himself to be the Almighty; and books have been written within the last twenty years in which this view is advocated.[1]

But, if we accept this latter hypothesis, we must retrace the whole of the path by which we have come, and revise our whole preliminary estimate of him. Indeed, my friend in the train would have to re-consider even the assumptions which he granted me. If the Power behind the universe is capable of playing such a sardonic joke upon mankind as to raise one distraught to the loftiest pinnacle in history, then we are at once deprived of all grounds for supposing it to be good, loving, merciful or even rational. It is not too much to say that if the supreme figure of history was mad, then the universe itself is mad, and life is not worth living—a conclusion which would end all further argument, as it would obviously be of no use to argue about anything.

OWEVER, I think I may safely assume that anyone who has troubled to read so far will agree with me that life is worth living; and we can, therefore, develop our argument in an optimistic spirit. If the universe is rational—if human history shows

[1] See A. Schweitzer, *Die psychiatrische Beurteilung Jesu*, for an account and a severe criticism of these books.

Theological Formulation 25

the guidance of conscious intelligence, and is not a mere crazy pattern ceaselessly turned out by a loom operated by a madman—then Jesus is God's supreme Messenger to humanity; and if he is God's supreme Messenger, the presumption is that his message about himself must be true; and if he claims, as we know from the documents that he did claim, a limitless authority over men's bodies and souls, and a mysterious and unique filial relation to God the Father, it would seem that those claims must be accepted.

And, given the acceptance of the claim, the subsequent development of Christian theology may not unreasonably be said to have been inevitable. It was inevitable that the immediate followers of Jesus should not merely describe him, on the basis of their own experience, as 'a man approved of God' (*Acts* ii. 22); 'the holy Servant of the Lord' (*Acts* iv. 27); 'anointed with the Spirit' (*Acts* x. 38); but also, on the basis of his own claims, should have proclaimed him as 'Lord of all' (*Acts* x. 36). St. Paul is only underlining this latter phrase when he describes Christ as 'God over all' (*Rom.* ix. 5); and the universal, almost startlingly placid acquiescence with which his explanation of the heavenly being of Christ in terms of 'pre-existence' and 'equality with God' was accepted by Christendom at large—contrasting as it does with the furious protests evoked from the

26 Theological Formulation

Jewish Christians by his attitude towards circumcision and the Law—irresistibly suggests that his doctrine of Christ was no new invention or importation from heathenism, but merely the intellectual formulation of that which was the recognized, original, instinctive belief of the Christian Church from the first.

Equally natural was it that St. John should have made explicit what is implicit in St. Paul's teaching, by borrowing (whether from Greek philosophy or Jewish Rabbinism matters not) the idea of the Logos, the cosmic Word or Thought of God, to express the divine being of Jesus, and his eternal inherence in, and eternal distinction from, the Father; and that these guiding thoughts should have been developed by the Councils and Fathers of the Catholic Church, in such a way that the great conception of his divine Sonship, revealed by our Lord to his original disciples by implication and parable, in undefined outlines, stands before us to-day, finally thought out, defined, and made precise, in the careful language of the second paragraph of the Nicene Creed and the last half of the Athanasian Creed.

It is not in the least surprising that there was a steady development in the doctrine of the Person of Christ between the first century and the fourth, from which latter our Nicene Creed dates—a development both of terminology, and, to a certain extent, of idea.

Theological Formulation 27

The impact of our Lord's personality upon the world was too tremendous and too blinding to be apprehended at once: it required time for its adequate study and description; and the process of arriving at the best formulation of the truth, by eliminating false and one-sided attempts to express it, was worked out through storms of controversy and amidst much that was not altogether edifying in the words and deeds of champions on either side.

But, if we abstract from the accidental traces of 'all-too-human' infirmity which the first few centuries of Christian history bear, and consider the development solely in itself, we shall find it very difficult indeed, and in fact impossible without recourse to an arbitrary *tour de force*, to impugn the continuity and inevitability of the process whereby the fully-developed Catholic doctrine of Christ was evolved out of the teaching of St. Paul and St. John; that teaching was but the philosophical formulation of the belief in the universal Lordship of Jesus held by the primitive Christian community; and that again flowed naturally from the vast and mysterious claims recorded by our most ancient and reliable sources as having been made (doubtless for the most part in private, and by hint and implication, but at the same time really made) by the historic Jesus himself.

We can see, too, by the mere light of human reasoning, and quite apart from the faith

28 Theological Formulation

which all Catholics have in the supernatural guidance of the Church, that the various heresies which the early Councils condemned, were, in fact, intrinsically condemnable, as failing to do justice either to the fullness of Christ's supernatural claim, or to the reality of his human nature. We are not likely now to have much sympathy with theories which maintain that Christ's body was a mere phantasm, or that the human Jesus and the divine Son were two separate persons, linked together in a kind of moral partnership. If the Christology which proclaims Christ to be divine is admissible at all—and we have seen the only alternative—then there is no serious rival to the Catholic Christology.

The language of the creeds has indeed been criticized on the ground that it is too metaphysical and abstract for the ordinary man; but this is not borne out by the practical experience of Christian teachers. The statement that Jesus Christ is one Person, possessing two natures, divine and human, can be taken in by any reasonably intelligent child. The phrase 'being of one substance,' or 'consubstantial,' in the Nicene Creed, does, perhaps, require some technical training in order to the apprehension of its full historical significance; but the most uninstructed Christian can grasp its essential meaning, namely, that Jesus is the same God and Lord as the Jehovah of the Old Testament.

God's Love

It would thus seem that, given the acceptance of the claim contained in *St. Matt.* xi. 27, there is no half-way house at which we can stop, short of the full belief of the Catholic Church. *Aut deus, aut vesanus.* We must take one road or the other. Why not follow the road of optimism, of faith, and of hope? Choose boldly that view which follows from the rationality of God in the universe, and throw yourself unreservedly into the full, pulsing life, the ever-glowing victorious faith, of historical and Catholic Christianity.

ERHAPS our friend in the train may reply: 'Well, you have led me on very skilfully from belief in Christ as a great and good man, to belief in him as the unique Messenger of God, and from that to his claim to be the Son of God, in an exalted but undefined sense, and from that again to the full Christology of the Church and the creeds; but I must confess that I still hesitate. I cannot, perhaps, justify it logically, but I have a feeling that this is all just a little bit too good to be true—such a supremely consoling and glorious an event as God becoming man is too wonderful a thing to happen in this drab, weary, workaday world.'

I do not pretend to be able, nor, I believe, is any man able, by mere reasoning, to kindle the light of faith, the noon-day certitude of conviction, in any other human soul: that must be done by God, either by direct illumination or by bringing the seeker after truth into contact with those who already have the flame burning within their souls. Reason cannot itself kindle the flame; it cannot do more than clear the ground and accumulate materials for the fire: as a modern divine has penetratingly said: ' Religion is not a thing that people can be argued into; it must be caught, like the measles, from those who have already got it.'

But I can at least conclude with one counter-question to the point last raised, namely this—Is anything too good to be true of God? If God is infinite, that is to say, if he is God at all, he must be infinite in his goodness; and the condescension of the Incarnation is not too much for that.

In fact, the Christian creed is the only one which does adequate justice to this infinite quality of God's love. In all other religions God is said to have sent messengers, but in historic Christianity God has come himself in person; and the consequences which flow from this idea are all characterized by the same congruity with the infinitude of God. The Incarnation provides an inexhaustible satisfaction for the hero-worshipping instinct. It presents us with the figure of one who is really man, yet may be given that unlimited

God's Love

adoration which we instinctively long to give to some one of our own race, but which no one who is merely man and nothing more could ever have deserved. In the Incarnation, too, is rooted the whole sacramental system, whereby the Redeemer penetrates the inmost recesses of our being with his divine life, and progressively transforms us into himself, slowly eliminating the flaws, the weaknesses, and the diseases of our souls. Through the Incarnation we know that God now has something which even his omniscience had not before, namely, a genuine human experience and memories.

All the comfort, all the attractiveness, and all the beauty of the Catholic system, with its sacraments and its worship, its gracious figures of Christ's Mother and his saints, and the mysterious atmosphere of its temples, which, with delicate, almost impalpable touches, soothes and subdues the stubborn will; all radiates and streams from the burning Heart of the God-Man, Jesus Christ, 'the same yesterday, to-day, and for ever.' If you have it not, pray that this final consummation may be added to you, this touch of the divine fire of faith, that so, in life and in death, you may be able to make your own the words of one of the greatest and best of Englishmen (W. E. Gladstone): 'All I write, and all I think, and all I hope, is based upon the divinity of our Lord, the one central hope of our poor, wayward race.'

THE CONGRESS BOOKS: No. 5

THE
VIRGIN BIRTH

C. B. MOSS
Assistant Priest of
St. Bartholomew's,
Dublin

LONDON
THE SOCIETY OF
SS. PETER & PAUL
32 George St., Hanover Sq., W. 1, and
The Abbey House, Westminster, S.W. 1

The Virgin Birth

God is born of maiden fair :
Mary doth the Saviour bear,
    Mary ever pure.

THE words of this old carol proclaim what Christians in every age have always believed. When the everlasting Son of God took to himself a human body and a human soul, and was born as a little baby in an eastern village, in order to save mankind, his birth was different from that of all other children, in two ways : first, he was free from the least flaw or taint of sin, and secondly, he had no human father, for God the Holy Ghost gave to his mother, though a virgin, the power to bear this child, and he was made man by the creative energy of God.

We have two accounts that describe some of the circumstances attending his birth: one in the gospel according to St. Luke, and the other in the gospel according to St. Matthew. St. Luke's account is as follows (i. 26–ii. 21) : ' The angel Gabriel was sent from God unto a city of Galilee named Nazareth, to a virgin betrothed to a man whose name was Joseph, of the house of David : and the virgin's name was Mary. And the angel came in unto her, and said, Hail, thou that art highly favoured, the Lord is with thee : blessed art thou among women. . . . And behold, thou shalt conceive in thy womb, and bring forth a son, and shalt call his name Jesus. . . . Then said Mary unto the angel, How shall this be, seeing I know not a man ? And the angel answered and said unto her : The Holy Ghost shall come upon thee, and the power of the Highest shall overshadow thee ; therefore also that holy thing which shall be born of thee shall be called the Son of God. . . . And Mary said, Behold the handmaid of the Lord : be it unto me according to thy word.'

A little later 'there went out a decree from Caesar Augustus, that all the world (*i.e.* Roman Empire) should be enrolled. And all went to be enrolled, every one into his own city. And Joseph also went up from Galilee, out of the city of Nazareth, into Judaea, unto the city of David, which is called Bethlehem ; (because he was of the house and lineage of David :) to enrol himself with Mary his betrothed wife, being great with child. And so it was, that while they were there the days were accomplished that she should be delivered. And she brought forth her firstborn son, and wrapped him in swaddling clothes, and laid him in a manger ; because there was no room for them in the inn.'

The Evidence Criticized

The other account is as follows (*St. Matt.* i. 18 ff.) : ' Now the birth of Jesus Christ was on this wise : When his mother Mary was betrothed to Joseph, before they came together, she was found with child of the Holy Ghost. Then Joseph her husband, being a just man, and not willing to make her a public example, was minded to put her away privily. But while he thought on these things, behold the angel of the Lord appeared to him in a dream, saying, Joseph, thou son of David, fear not to take unto thee Mary thy wife : for that which is conceived in her is of the Holy Ghost. And she shall bring forth a son, and thou shalt call his name Jesus, for he shall save his people from their sins. . . . Then Joseph being raised from sleep, did as the angel of the Lord had bidden him, and took unto him his wife ; and knew her not till she had brought forth her firstborn son : and he called his name Jesus.'

FOR many people the fact that this story is told in the gospels, especially when its subject is of such vast importance as the birth of the Son of God, is enough to convince them of its truth. But it is necessary, in an age when nothing is free from criticism, to ask what scientific value our evidence bears

6 The Evidence Criticized

in support of the statement that our Lord was born of a virgin; and to answer this question we must treat the gospels for the time being as if they were just ordinary records of events in past history.

We find that our two accounts, while agreeing as to the main facts that our Lord was born at Bethlehem, and that he had no human father, are quite independent of one another. St. Luke tells the story of the angel Gabriel's message to the blessed Virgin, the journey to Bethlehem for the enrolment, the birth of our Lord in the stable, and certain other events, most of which would have had a special interest for the women friends of the blessed Virgin. On the other hand, the account in *St. Matthew* includes the story of St. Joseph's dream, the visit of the wise men, the flight into Egypt, and the return to Nazareth, told from the point of view of St. Joseph. This account may have been preserved by 'the Lord's brethren' (probably sons of St. Joseph by an earlier marriage), and given by them to the evangelist.

The two accounts do not anywhere tell the same story: yet they are consistent with one another. More than that, they explain one another. If we had not got the account in *St. Matthew*, the point of view of St. Joseph would be unknown. If we had not got St. Luke's account, we should not understand how the Holy Family came to be at Bethlehem

The Evidence Criticized   7

at all. Both accounts evidently belong to the time when it was still possible to be both a Jew by religion and a Christian, which is a proof of their early date; and both bear the unmistakable stamp of truth, as we may easily see if we compare them with the strange and ludicrous legends of the 'apocryphal gospels' which grew up after our four gospels were written.

The agreement of two very early and yet independent accounts of an event is the strongest kind of evidence we could have. And St. Luke at any rate was an educated man of science, not at all likely to accept stories without sufficient evidence. He tells us himself that he had 'perfect understanding of everything from the very first'; and we know that he was in Palestine not later than A.D. 57 (*Acts* xxi. 17), probably for two years, when he must have had every opportunity of hearing the facts from many who had known the blessed Virgin herself, including St. James the 'brother' of our Lord. Regarded simply as an historical fact, the Virgin Birth of our Lord rests on evidence better than we have for many important facts in ancient history which nobody dreams of questioning.

But why is not the Virgin Birth mentioned by St. Mark, St. John, or St. Paul ? It was outside the plan of their writings. Neither St. Mark nor St. John gives any account of our Lord's infancy. But it is pretty clear that

8   The Evidence Criticized

both of them knew that our Lord had no human father. St. Mark makes the people of Nazareth say: ' Is not this the carpenter ? ' whereas in *St. Matthew* the words are ' Is not this the carpenter's son ? ' and in *St. Luke,* ' Is not this Joseph's son ? ' St. John's gospel was written much later, and assumes that its readers know the other three: many people think that the words ' which were born, not of blood, nor of the will of the flesh, nor of the will of man, but of God ' (*St. John* i. 13), are an allusion to the Virgin Birth.

As for St. Paul, it is impossible that he did not know what was known to his intimate friend and companion St. Luke. Besides, he teaches quite plainly that our Lord was in heaven before his birth, and that he is truly God. And there is no instance in ancient times of any one who accepted these two doctrines and yet did not believe in the Virgin Birth. As a matter of fact, St. Paul never mentions Nazareth or Capernaum or indeed any feature of our Lord's Galilean ministry: so that if his silence is regarded as a proof against the accuracy of our information about Christ's birth, it might also be taken as a proof that Christ never healed the sick or preached the gospel to the poor.

There is no evidence whatever on the other side. No early Christian writer, either within or outside the New Testament, takes any other view of our Lord's birth, than that he was

The Evidence Criticized

born of a virgin. St. Ignatius, bishop of Antioch (martyred about A.D. 110) calls the Virgin Birth one of the three 'mysteries of shouting,' which are known to all Christians. We have proof that it was believed in the second century by the churches of Syria, Egypt, Greece, Italy, Gaul, and North Africa, and that no Christian ever thought of doubting it. From (probably) A.D. 150 it formed part of the creed in which every Christian professed his belief at baptism. In later ages it was even accepted by some who refused to believe that Jesus Christ is God. Paul of Samosata in the third century, Mohammed in the seventh (and through him all Mohammedans), and Socinus, the founder of 'Unitarianism,' in the sixteenth, all admitted that our Lord was born of a virgin, though they denied his Godhead.

We believe, therefore, in the Virgin Birth of our Lord, both because God has revealed it to us in the Bible, supported by the universal tradition of the Church, and because there is ample evidence for it as an historical fact.

But the creed is not a collection of statements which have no connexion with one another. It is a chain of which every link fits into its place in the great scheme of the Catholic faith. And so, while we dare not say that God could not have become man by being born of two human parents, we can insist that his birth of a virgin fully agrees

10 Objections Considered

with the rest of his plan for the salvation of men.

Our Lord Jesus Christ is, like us, human: he is also, unlike us, everlasting God. Like us, he took his human nature from a human mother: unlike us, since he existed already in heaven, he needed no human father.

Moreover, it was necessary, if our Lord was to save us from sin, that he himself should be free from that taint which all of us have received with the many other elements of our fallen nature from our parents, and yet should be fully and truly man. Through being 'conceived by the Holy Ghost,' in a manner different from ordinary men, he escaped from this taint with which all other human beings are born, which is called 'original sin.' Thus the Virgin Birth, no less than the Cross and the Empty Tomb, was part of God's plan for our salvation.

OBJECTIONS to the doctrine of the Virgin Birth appear to be of two kinds:

(i) It is argued by some persons that legends of the virgin birth of heroes are found in many nations: and that the story of the birth of Jesus Christ is but another legend of the same kind. This argument seems a strange one. We might as well say that because there is a legend about the Babes in the Wood, who were supposed to have been murdered by their uncle, therefore Richard III did not murder his nephews, the Princes in the Tower.

But as a matter of fact no such legend can be found either among the Hebrews or in any nation with which they were in contact. The famous passage in *Isai.* vii., ' Behold, a virgin shall conceive and bear a son, and shall call his name Immanuel,' was not understood by the Jews to refer to a virgin birth, and was never applied to the Messiah by any one before St. Matthew's gospel was written, any more than the verse of *Hosea*, ' Out of Egypt have I called my son,' was ever regarded as a prophecy that the Messiah would arise out of Egypt. Both passages have quite a different meaning in the Old Testament. And if the Jews had believed that the Messiah would be born of a virgin, they would have continued to believe it, as they did continue to believe that he would be born at Bethlehem.

The heathen legends of imaginary events which are sometimes compared with the Virgin Birth are of such a low moral tone, to put it mildly, that it is incredible that they could have influenced the strict Jewish circle from which the story of our Lord's birth, as told in the gospels, is derived. The legend of the supernatural birth of Gautama, the founder of Buddhism (who lived about 500 B.C.), is

12 Objections Considered

much later than the Christian era, and is possibly due in some of its features to the influence of Christianity; in any case, there is not the least trace of Buddhist influence in the New Testament. The exaltation of virginity was not at all in accordance with Jewish belief and feeling; and the fact that nevertheless the story of our Lord's birth of a virgin is clearly Jewish through and through is a strong proof of its truth.

(ii) But the real objection, in many minds, to the doctrine of the Virgin Birth is that it involves a miracle. This is not the place to discuss the question of miracles. But it is clear that the miracles cannot be torn out of the gospels. If miracles are impossible, the gospels are utterly untrustworthy. And, after all, if you believe that the eternal and almighty God, by whom all things were made, who guides the stars in their courses, and in whom all things exist from hour to hour, was born on this earth as a helpless baby, and lived as a man among men, and died the death of a criminal, then you cannot complain of the difficulty of the Virgin Birth. Compared with that most stupendous of miracles, the Virgin Birth is but a detail. And that miracle of the Incarnation is the very centre of the Christian religion, the foundation of all that can be called Christian, in morals as well as in doctrine.

The 'Mother of God' 13

N conclusion, we may consider why the Church calls the blessed Virgin Mary 'Mother of God.' In the fifth century there was an archbishop of Constantinople, named Nestorius, who taught, or at any rate was accused of teaching, that Jesus Christ was not God to begin with, but that the Word of God descended upon him, so that he became God. Nestorius said, 'I cannot call a three-months-old infant God.' So a general council of the Church was held at Ephesus, in A.D. 431, which declared that the blessed Virgin Mary was rightly called 'Mother of God' (in Greek, *Theotokos*), in order to show that our Lord Jesus Christ, from the very first moment of his existence as man, was truly God, the second Person of the holy Trinity.

This decree was accepted by every part of the Church, with the one exception of the Assyrian Church of the further East, which was separated by political difficulties from the rest of the Church; and even the Assyrian Church may be said to have accepted the decree of Ephesus indirectly, for it has accepted the authority of the later Council of Chalcedon, which recognized that of Ephesus.

When we say that the blessed Virgin is Mother of God, we do not, of course, mean that she is the source of his divine nature: that is an idea too absurd and blasphemous to need refutation. We mean that she is the

14 The 'Mother of God'

mother of Jesus Christ as man, and that Jesus Christ, who was born of her, is, and always was, truly God; and that therefore his mother is the mother of God. It is impossible to deny this without denying either that our Lord is truly God, or that he truly became man.

We know absolutely nothing certain about the life of our Lord's mother except what is told us in the gospels and in the Acts of the Apostles. But what we do know about her is enough to teach us that she is the most glorious of all created beings: for it was she whom God prepared to be the means by which he should be born into the world: and it is she whom he has placed in a closer relationship to himself than any other creature, nearer than any angel or archangel, in that he has made her his mother.

> Mother and maiden
>   Was never none but she.
> Well may such a Lady
>   God's mother be.

THE CONGRESS BOOKS: No. 6

THE RESURRECTION OF CHRIST

B. T. D. SMITH
*Fellow of Sidney Sussex College,
Cambridge; Examining Chaplain
to the Bishop of Lichfield*

LONDON
THE SOCIETY OF
SS. PETER & PAUL
32 *George St., Hanover Sq., W.* 1, *and
The Abbey House, Westminster, S.W.* 1

The Resurrection of Christ

THERE is one article of the Christian creed that few will be prepared to deny—the statement that our Lord was 'crucified under Pontius Pilate.' Yet the amazing fact confronts us that Christianity survived the tragedy of Good Friday.

Those who had brought about Christ's condemnation and had watched his execution, might well have been convinced that with his death they had witnessed the death of any movement connected with him. Nothing could have seemed more probable. His disciples were broken men. Their faith and hope in Christ, if not their love for him, were buried in his grave. Nevertheless, it is quite certain that in a few weeks' time those same disciples, with faith and love and hope newborn and radiant, preached Jesus as Lord and Saviour, and so changed the course of human history.

All this we know. But it is well first to remind ourselves how startling are the facts, that we may realize how overwhelming must have been the conviction that explains them,

Our Authorities

the belief that the Crucified had risen from the dead.

It is not only because present-day Christianity owes to this belief its very existence that the story of Christ's resurrection is a matter of direct and practical importance to every thoughtful man. The Easter faith that Christ has risen carries with it an answer to the two great questions that have ever perplexed men's minds: the problem of death and the problem of evil.

For the Christian, death is robbed, not of its mystery, but of its terrors. The problem of evil, with the doubt it raises as to either the power or the goodness of God (a doubt which is only deepened if the life of Jesus Christ closed on the cross), is lifted from our hearts if God raised him from the dead. In that act we shall see the proof that Goodness is immortal and Love invincible, the promise of the final overthrow of all evil, the assurance of the ultimate triumph of God.

The question then that becomes urgent for all of us is this: Upon what evidence does the belief in Christ's resurrection rest, and is that evidence worthy of trust? The more we recognize the magnitude of the issues involved, the more eagerly shall we ask the question. An attempt is made in the following pages to supply an answer.

The first Christians based their belief primarily upon the testimony of men and women who claimed to have seen and heard the risen Christ.

To-day we are separated from them by many centuries, and must depend for our knowledge of the facts to which they bore witness upon certain of the New Testament writings. We must try to estimate the value of these records. The New Testament writings that chiefly concern us are the following:

(*a*) The first epistle to the Corinthians, written by St. Paul about the year A.D. 54. In this letter the apostle gives a short account of the facts about the Resurrection, as they had been imparted to him after his conversion (probably within two or three years of the events related), and as he himself had taught his converts (1 *Cor.* xv. 1-11). Here we have a very early list of the resurrection appearances: not a complete one, but limited to those which would be most impressive and convincing when quoted as evidence: that is, appearances to the apostolic body; to outstanding individuals in the early Church (Peter the leader of the apostles, James the head of the church in Jerusalem); to a very large gathering of disciples.

(*b*) The Gospel according to St. Mark was composed not later than A.D. 60-70. Most students of the gospels would agree to the following statements: that it was actually written by the man whose name it bears: that it is based, as tradition asserts, upon

Our Authorities

the personal memories of St. Peter, whom Mark accompanied upon his travels : and that it is an historical record of very great value. Mark, though not one of Christ's original followers, enjoyed special opportunities for getting information about the gospel story In the early days of the Church his mother's house, at Jerusalem, formed a meeting place for the disciples (*Acts* xii. 12) ; while he was closely connected not only with St. Peter (1 *Pet.* v. 13), but with St. Paul (*Acts* xii. 25, etc., *Coloss.* iv. 10, *Philem.* 24, 2 *Tim.* iv. 11).

Unfortunately we have almost certainly lost the conclusion of this book. Verses 9-20 of the last chapter represent an attempt made at a later date to supply a suitable ending (see marginal note in the Revised Version). That is to say, we have only got St. Mark's account of the Resurrection as far as the flight of the women from the tomb. But it is very probable that some portion at least of the original conclusion is still to be found in the first of our gospels.

(*c*) The Gospel according to St. Matthew, written by a Jewish Christian about A.D. 60-80, is thought to owe its title to the fact that its author made large use of an earlier work compiled by Matthew the apostle. In his final chapters, as indeed throughout the book, the writer is using St. Mark's gospel as one of his main sources of information. It is, therefore, extremely likely that he is continuing to draw upon St. Mark's narrative for part of the material in chapter xxviii. 9-20, and that in this way some of Mark's lost ending is preserved for us.

(*d*) It may be asserted with a considerable degree of confidence that the third of our gospels and the Acts of the Apostles are the work of a Greek physician and companion of St. Paul, Luke by name, and that the writer is entitled to high rank as an historian. He seems to have had access to special sources of information with regard to events in Jerusalem and the early days of the Church there. This is not surprising when we remember that he accompanied St. Paul on his last journey to Jerusalem, and remained in Palestine until Paul was sent a prisoner to Rome.

(*e*) As so much remains in dispute both as to the authorship and the historical character of the Gospel according to St. John, we will not prejudice the argument by using it save as a secondary source of information.

Our conclusions then are these : The accounts of the resurrection of our Lord are contained in early documents. Of their writers Paul, Mark, and Luke could obtain information at firsthand and from many different sources.

The Evidence Considered 7

THE first important point for us to notice is that the Resurrection is dated. All through the Christian tradition, however much it may differ in details, runs the statement still preserved in our creeds: 'On the third day he rose again.'

This seems to rule out at once the idea that belief in Christ's resurrection grew up gradually, as the awful scenes of his crucifixion were blotted out of the minds of the disciples after their return to Galilee by happier memories of earlier days spent with Christ as their Friend and Master; and that the revival of their faith created the conviction that the grave could not hold him. All such theories founder on the certain fact that the Christian tradition unanimously traces back the beginning of the Easter faith to a date so close to the Crucifixion as the third day, which must mean, moreover, that whatever happened on that date occurred in Jerusalem itself, the very scene of the tragedy.

What did happen on the third day? Very early that morning, so the gospels state, women who had followed Christ from Galilee to Jerusalem visited his sepulchre. They found the tomb open, and the body gone: while supernatural experiences conveyed to them the unexpected, barely-comprehended gospel of the resurrection.

With the exception that the Fourth Evange-

8 The Evidence Considered

list confines himself to the story of one of the women, the tradition preserved in the gospels is unanimous on these points. It will not surprise us, remembering all the circumstances, if the accounts do not tally word for word.

That the disciples, when the women returned to them, and however they received their strange story, would take steps to verify that part of it which could be tested—the condition of the tomb—is altogether probable, quite apart from the evidence of our records (*St. Luke* xxiv. 24, compare *St. John* xx. 3).

It has been suggested, however, in recent years that it is not necessary to accept the story of the Empty Tomb in order to believe whole-heartedly that Jesus Christ is alive for evermore—and that he rose from the dead 'with all things appertaining to the perfection of man's nature.'

Such a presentation of the Easter message, whatever attractions it may have for those who find the 'miraculous' element in the narrative a difficulty, cannot be paralleled from the New Testament. This is certain, that belief in Christ's resurrection and belief that his tomb was empty were inseparably united in the faith of the apostles, and that the Jewish opponents of Christianity could have dealt a staggering if not a mortal blow to that faith by producing the body of the dead Christ. That they failed to do so is

The Evidence Considered 9

perhaps the strongest evidence for the truth of this part of the tradition. They could only circulate such stories as St. Matthew ascribes to them, alleging fraud on the part of the disciples.

If, as the apostles assert, the body of Christ saw no corruption, then in raising his Son from the dead God remained true to his sacramental method of revelation, and gave an outward sign as surety and proof of his truth and grace.

At this point we must face an apparent conflict of tradition. We have seen that St. Mark's narrative now closes with the flight of the women from the tomb. But he has already stated that they had received a message for the disciples, to the effect that the risen Christ would appear to them in Galilee. St. Matthew tells the same story, following St. Mark's narrative. He does not describe what took place when the women returned to the apostles, but, after relating the Jewish explanation of the empty tomb, proceeds: 'But the eleven disciples went into Galilee, unto the mountain where Jesus had appointed them.' If we had only St. Matthew's gospel we should know of no appearances of Christ to his apostles outside Galilee: and might assume that they returned there straightway.

If, on the other hand, we had only the Gospel according to St. Luke, we should know of no appearances outside Jerusalem. In

10 The Evidence Considered

this gospel the message to the apostles is that they should remember what Christ had told them in Galilee, that he would rise again; and the appearances which St. Luke relates all take place at or in the neighbourhood of Jerusalem.

This difficulty is not really so formidable as it may appear at first sight.

(*a*) We must remember that the evangelists are writing to meet their own needs, not ours. Their purpose is not to write a complete account of all that happened before the Ascension; they are selecting such incidents as best serve their own very practical purposes.

(*b*) Another factor which determined the contents of their gospels was that of space They must obviously set some limit to the size of their books; and as they drew near the close of their narratives it is more than probable that they would compress their story if possible within the limits of the roll of writing material they were then engaged upon. Their 'volumes' were paper rolls of strictly limited length.

With these two considerations in mind let us look again at the closing narratives of the gospels of St. Matthew and of St. Luke. Both of them show signs of compression, and this is very obvious in the case of St. Matthew. He has selected but one appearance of Christ to the disciples, and he has told that very summarily. There is no difficulty

The Resurrection Appearances 11

in supposing that some of the many appearances omitted by him took place outside Galilee.

St. Luke too has had to select and to abbreviate. He had access to special sources of information in regard to the Jerusalem appearances (see above p. 6). He decided, therefore, to omit all references to the appearances in Galilee, that he might find room for these narratives. Even with this omission he has only space to tell in a few lines all that took place after the first Easter Sunday, so that the reader might easily suppose that verses 44-53 of chapter xxiv. belong to the same occasion as the preceding narrative. But it is the author himself who tells us, at the opening of his second volume (*Acts* i. 3) that these nine verses cover a period of forty days, during which the risen Christ appeared to the disciples and instructed them 'concerning the kingdom of God.' There is then ample room here for the Galilean appearances.

WE turn, therefore, to the question, how did the disciples receive the story brought them by the women?

St. Luke tells us that it seemed to them 'nonsense,' the product of delirium. That surely is what we should expect: they

12 The Resurrection Appearances

were too bankrupt of hope to risk anything on such a tale. Yet it increases our respect for the honesty of the narrative when we find that no attempt is made to cloak the apostles' lack of faith. If investigation proved that the tomb was indeed empty, that could be explained by the malice of the Jews.

But even their despair had to give place to uncertainty as evidence for the incredible truth accumulated. Before the day was over, Peter their leader had seen with his own eyes the risen Christ: this was placed first in the list of appearances received by St. Paul (*St. Luke* xxiv. 34, 1 *Cor.* xv. 5). Late that night two disciples came back from a neighbouring village, to say that Christ had joined them on the road, and that he was made known to them in the breaking of bread. It was then that he himself stood in the midst of his apostles, and doubt gave place to Easter joy.

According to St. John's gospel, the disciples remained in Jerusalem at least another week; for he relates that it was on the following Sunday that Thomas, absent on the former occasion, was at length convinced. And we may assume that it was on one or other of these occasions that our Lord made that appointment with the apostles in Galilee of which St. Matthew speaks (*St. Matt.* xxviii. 16).

The appointed meeting-place was a mountain-side. St. Matthew's words suggest that those assembled there saw our Lord before

The Resurrection Appearances 13

he came to them (compare verses 17 and 18) ; and that while the Eleven had no doubt as to the identity of the approaching figure, and worshipped, some stood uncertain until he drew near and spoke to them. Others then were present besides the apostles, and we may reasonably connect this appearance with that recorded by St. Paul as made to above five hundred brethren at once, of whom the greater part were still alive when he wrote, some twenty-five years later. Only in Galilee would so large a number of 'brethren' be found.

Probably Galilee also was the scene of another appearance mentioned by St. Paul, that to James the Lord's brother: a reference that helps us to understand how it came about that while the Lord's brethren are represented in the gospels as standing aloof from him, in the Acts they are believers, James becoming the head of the church in Jerusalem. Galilee, again, is the scene of an appearance to the apostles recorded in the Fourth Gospel (*St. John* xxi).

The apostles' homes were in Galilee. It was natural therefore that they should return to that district; and, as we have seen, we have strong evidence that they did do so. But it is equally certain that before Pentecost they were again assembled at Jerusalem. There it was, according to St. Luke, that the Lord appeared to them, bidding them tarry in the city until they were clothed

14 The Resurrection Appearances

with power from on high (*St. Luke* xxiv. 49). We may perhaps identify this appearance with that 'to all the apostles' mentioned by St. Paul before he closes his list with that last appearance on the Damascus Road to Saul the persecutor.

We have now passed the different strands of the Christian tradition under review. No attempt has been made to conceal the fact that our records are fragmentary and incomplete. They do not tell the same story in the same words. But the very diversity of the traditions makes their essential unity the more impressive. So far from cancelling out, they complete one another.

The gospel of the Resurrection dates back to a time when the birth of a legend based on simple credulity or the happy optimism of an untried faith is impossible. We see a belief establishing itself in spite of the distrust and suspicion of men already once bitterly disillusioned. The evidence comes to us from many quarters, from many differing types of character. We hear of manifestations to individuals, to small groups, and to large; but not in that fixed order. There is no suggestion that these experiences originated with the few, and then under the contagious influence of excitement spread to the many. Such a theory indeed breaks down in face of the plain fact that the manifestations ceased just when the period of

Verified by Human Experience 15

intense spiritual and emotional stress began for the disciples with the day of Pentecost.

We are confronted then with the evidence of those who assert simply and soberly that they have both seen and spoken to Jesus Christ raised from the dead; not in ecstatic vision, but as a man meets and speaks with his friend.

There are many events in history received without question that are not so well attested as the resurrection of Jesus Christ.

BUT the evidence for the truth of this belief does not end, as indeed it does not begin, with the records we have investigated. For, however strong the historical evidence for the fact of the Resurrection may be, it will only carry full weight with the man who is prepared to grant the possibility of divine revelation within human history, of divine activities which give birth to unique events. And the story of the Resurrection forms part of a large context, itself claiming to be the record of such a revelation made by God to men. This record covers the history of the chosen people, and it leads up to and culminates in the story of that Life which is said to have triumphed over death in order to become the source of new life to all the human race. We cannot isolate the miracle of the

16 Verified by Human Experience

Resurrection from the miracle of the historic life of Jesus of Nazareth, and so pass judgement upon it. Consider this event, admittedly unique, as part of that unique life, and, so the Christian claims, it will be seen to fall into place, to harmonize with its context.

Nor does our evidence stop short there. It takes in the story of the new movement in human society which dates from the first Easter and Pentecost, the history of the Christian Church down to our own day. Here the record is continued of 'the things which Jesus began both to do and to teach.' It is the story of the achievements of the risen Christ. If it is a tale of failure as well as of success, the failure is that of the human material with which he works, and does but serve to set in higher relief the miracles of his power, the evidence that a new supernatural life is operative within the world.

If history confirms the gospel of the Resurrection, it is the personal experience of the believer that verifies it. Faith rightly asks for evidence that will justify her adventure, but evidence cannot accompany her to her journey's end. The point must be reached where she must press forward alone into the unseen, where Christ is seated on the right hand of God. But we are compassed about with a great cloud of witnesses, who testify: 'Blessed are they that have not seen, and yet have believed.'

THE CONGRESS BOOKS: No. 7

THE ASCENSION

F. W. GREEN
Fellow of Merton College,
Oxford, Examining Chaplain
to the Bishop of Manchester

LONDON
THE SOCIETY OF
SS. PETER & PAUL
32 George St., Hanover Sq., W. 1, *and*
The Abbey House, Westminster, S.W. 1

The Ascension

BELIEF in the Ascension of our Lord into heaven is for Christians not only important but vital. If the Incarnation is the foundation of our faith, and the Resurrection the ground of our hope, the Ascension is the inspiration of our life and worship, indeed the very heart of their enthusiasm. It is the duty and privilege of Christians to preach Christ as Saviour, it is their glory to worship him as King. And in this perhaps we may detect one of the subtle yet profound differences between Catholicism and at any rate modern forms of Protestantism. Catholic feeling, Catholic art, and Catholic devotion are mainly concentrated not on the figure of the historic Jesus, utterly authoritative as that earthly life must always be, but on Christ exalted and reigning —reigning even from the cross. Touching and beautiful the picture of the '*Ecce Homo*' may be: but a stronger and a more triumphant faith has been the secret of Catholic courage and devotion, ever since the first martyr saw the heaven opened and the Son of Man standing at the right hand of God, or

The Historical Event 3

the seer of the *Revelation* saw in the living flame the glorified Humanity. The Ascension is more than merely a past event : it stands for an ever-present fact.

An event nevertheless it was ; and it is just here that there are difficulties which must be honestly faced if we are to be always ready to give an answer for the hope that is in us.

Although the Bible several times mentions the last appearance of our Lord on earth, there is, strictly speaking, only one full account of his Ascension. It is true that St. Mark's gospel records the fact that he was received up into heaven and sat down on the right hand of God : but this is hardly a description, the language is obviously figurative. And in any case the present ending of St. Mark's gospel, as indeed is well known, is an appendix substituted for the original ending, which was very early lost. The gospel according to St. Matthew gives an account of the last appearance in Galilee and the great commission of our Lord to his disciples, but says nothing about an ascension. (*St. Matt.* xxviii. 16.) St. John similarly describes an appearance by the shore of the Lake of Galilee, but he too says nothing of an ascension, except (characteristically) in two apparently casual references in other parts of his gospel (*St. John* vi. 62 ; xx. 17). Only St. Luke describes the leave-taking on the Mount of Olives. ' He

4   The Historical Event

led them out as far as to Bethany and he lifted up his hands and blessed them ' (*St. Luke* xxiv. 50). But even then he does not describe anything that could be called an ascension. ' And it came to pass, while he blessed them, he was parted from them.' The words ' and was carried up into heaven ' are omitted in some of the most important manuscripts, and may, therefore, not be genuine.

It is only when we turn to St. Luke's second volume, the *Acts of the Apostles*, that we get anything like a description of an ascension. ' And when he had spoken these things, while they beheld, he was taken up ; and a cloud received him out of their sight. And while they looked steadfastly toward heaven as he went up, behold two men stood by them in white apparel, which also said, Ye men of Galilee, why stand ye gazing up into heaven ? This same Jesus which is taken up from you into heaven shall so come, in like manner as ye have seen him go into heaven ' (*Acts* i. 9). What seems to be meant is that the disciples, as they stood round, did actually behold our Lord's body lifted from the earth a certain distance, after which a cloud hid him. As the cloud floated or dissolved their eyes followed it, as though they were beholding the disappearance of Jesus into the region of the stars.

Now we know enough of the facts of nature and the physical structure of the universe to

The Historical Event 5

understand that Christ did not ascend to the region of the stars. Heaven is not a place situated above us in respect of geographical position; nor would anything be gained by his going from one planet to another. It is, however, quite reasonable to suppose that the physical elevation of our Lord's body off the earth, and its reception by the cloud, was a piece of symbolism; a sacrament or outward and visible sign of the inward truth that he had passed beyond the veil of all earthly sight, and had taken his glory. For the clouds, in the Bible, are regarded as the natural medium of communication between earth and heaven, as well as symbols of the veil which must needs be drawn between the frail perceptions of weak and sinful men, and the refulgent majesty of the glory of God. The event may in fact have happened in something like the way that Raphael, in his great picture, imagined Jesus to have appeared to the three disciples in the vision of the Transfiguration. In any case we may note the contrast evidently intended in this wonderful story with the record of the previous appearances of our Lord after his resurrection. The vanishing on this last occasion was different, inasmuch as it was gradual, deliberate, and final, 'as they were looking.' The process could be observed up to a certain point, then no more.

6 Its Scriptural Interpretation

SO ran the historical tradition; but this alone did not suffice to express the full belief of Christians. St. Paul saw Christ always in one blaze of glory. In the first ardour of his conversion, which never wholly faded from his mind, he could not distinguish between the glory of the Resurrection and the glory of the Ascension: they were one and the same thing to him. And it is probable that where St. Paul mentions the Resurrection he means to imply the Ascension with it, just as the references in the New Testament to Baptism imply Confirmation as another stage in one process.

But, as usual with St. Paul, we must look for his profoundest teaching on Christian doctrine in places where the lesson he wishes to impress is most practical. In the epistle to the Philippians he teaches humility by reference to our Lord's exaltation, which was the natural result of the experience of humiliation through which he had voluntarily passed. ' Wherefore God hath highly exalted him, and given him a name that is above every name, that at the name of Jesus every knee should bow' (*Philipp*. ii. 10). Similarly in the epistle to the Ephesians, to teach the lesson of unity among believers possessing spiritual endowments strangely varied and unequal, he explains the reason for that inequality by ascribing the gifts to the prodigal generosity

Its Scriptural Interpretation 7

of a triumphant conqueror. Using the words of the psalmist, he describes a triumphal procession winding up the newly conquered Hill of Zion. The figure is that of a victorious captain taking possession of the enemy's citadel, with his train of captives and spoil following him in triumph: the individual warrior is for the moment swallowed up in the glory of the occasion, and there is no room for the advancement of particular claims. 'When he ascended up on high, he led captivity captive and gave gifts unto men' (*Ephes.* iv. 8 ff.). Henceforth he showers upon his Church the gifts of the Holy Spirit in all their profuse abundance.

In neither of these passages, of course, is St. Paul giving a precise statement of Christian doctrine; they are important as allusions to a belief in the Ascension of Christ as being at once the inspiration to a life of Christian humility and patient toil, as well as the source and explanation of the power, grace, and authority inherent in the Church, which is the body of Christ. We too, in virtue of our incorporation in that body by Baptism, have been made 'to sit together in heavenly places in Christ Jesus' (*Ephes.* ii. 6).

The epistle to the Hebrews, which, though not written by St. Paul, yet has much of his spirit, has the same identification of the Resurrection and the Ascension as together making one great event with no logical interval

8 Its Scriptural Interpretation

between them. ' Who when he had by himself purged our sins, sat down on the right hand of the Majesty on high' (*Hebr.* i. 3). Christ's absolute exaltation to the highest position in the universe, whether in the suffering of his passion, or by his resurrection and ascension, is throughout this epistle made the supreme reason for claiming and holding the allegiance of men, who felt strongly the counter-attraction of a conservative appeal for loyalty to Judaism and the old faith. It is, moreover, the epistle to the Hebrews which tells us that as our High Priest who has passed into the heavens, Jesus Christ ever liveth to make intercession for us. (*Hebr.* vii. 25.)

We have not space here to speak of the imagery of the book of *Revelation*. We may note, however, the place of the Ascension in what appears to be a very ancient form of creed or hymn, quoted in the first epistle to Timothy : ' [God] was manifested in the flesh, justified in the Spirit ; seen of angels, preached unto the Gentiles ; believed on in the world, received up into glory ' (1 *Tim.* iii. 16). The New Testament writers taken as a whole may be said to regard the passion, resurrection, and ascension of Christ as steps in the process of his exaltation through suffering, ' as the absolute sacrifice of self which issued in the absolute triumph over the limitations of earthly existence ' (Westcott).

The Element of Symbolism 9

NOW it is quite clear that in all such passages from the *Acts* and the epistles the writers are largely using the language of symbolism. They make use, indeed, of a good deal of Jewish speculation about a Messiah ' coming with the clouds of heaven ' (*Dan.* vii. 13), about the ascent of the Blessed through the seven heavens to God, about the hierarchies of angels, thrones, principalities, and powers. But nothing is more absurd than the disparaging references of some teachers of our time to what is called the ' three-storey theology ' of the New Testament—the idea that the New Testament teaching depends upon the existence of a local and material heaven above the earth, and a local and material hell below it. Nothing indeed is more remarkable than the almost complete absence from the New Testament of anything of the sort. Dull readers may have understood the language, just as the dull critics have, in a stupid literal sense : but not so the writers. They are using symbols.

They could not in fact do otherwise. They knew as well as we do that absolute truth cannot be adequately expressed in human language. The difficulty comes not from the limitations of their knowledge, but from the nature of the event itself. Granted that our Lord did ascend to the right hand of God, still the words convey to us no detailed picture of

10 The Element of Symbolism

what that means. We can only know things through experience; all knowledge comes in that way. We can to a certain extent expand our experience, but only by the help of, and on the same lines as, the experience itself. That is exactly what is meant by faith—the extension of knowledge beyond experience; and a great deal of our life is lived upon that principle. But in the event which we are now considering, we assert, as the first Christians asserted, that our Lord has passed with his body far beyond all the limits of our present experience. He entered into other conditions; conditions which we hope to experience ourselves some day, but of which, short of that, we can have no possible conception. The words, therefore, in which we assert 'he ascended *into heaven*' (as if it were a geographical place), can convey nothing detailed to human imagination, for us who have so little insight into the realities to which they refer.[1]

Nevertheless, when we say the language is 'symbolical' we do not mean it is 'unreal.' A symbol in Christian theology has always meant something more than a mere sign. It has always had the meaning of a sacrament; an effectual sign in which the symbol partakes of the reality of the thing signified. And for

---

[1] In this they are, therefore, absolutely different from the words in which the creeds attest the Virgin Birth, which was an event in this world.

The Element of Symbolism 11

this reason we must not renounce our right to use earthly language about heavenly things. The Incarnation is our assurance that in using about the Ascension, or the Eucharist or any other mystery of the Catholic religion, the language of space and time, of flesh and blood, we are not distorting the reality or saying anything false. Rudimentary and incomplete as the impression may be which we are capable of receiving about divine realities, nevertheless the material means by which the reality is conveyed to us does not distort or misrepresent it, any more than the mechanism of sight distorts the images it conveys of the outside world. We are assured that God can sufficiently reveal his truth to us in the terms of human action, because he has revealed his own self to us in human flesh.

It is a mistake to turn away from the seen in order to realize the unseen. We are not to be frightened by either Modernists or Quakers from the bodily language of the Church's formulas, even when we cannot follow the words in our experience beyond a certain point. So in the Ascension of our Lord, when we say ' he went up,' and ' a cloud received him out of their sight,' that is the human form which the event must wear ; that was its natural expression for men. No amount of restatement will ever make any improvement upon it or bring us any nearer to the truth. And we may be quite certain

12 The Spiritual Meaning

that once we give up speaking of our Lord's Ascension in the way that simple people do, and as the New Testament describes it, we shall be in danger of losing some real portion of the reality. If we want to know what the Ascension means in its spiritual sense, we shall not arrive at it by dropping the material form in which it first made itself known—in the same language as the Incarnation.

ND what is the spiritual meaning of the Ascension? It can be stated summarily under two heads. It is the pledge of the fulfilment of human destiny; and it is the guarantee of the universal lordship and priesthood of Jesus.

First, then, mankind in the person of Jesus Christ has actually reached the goal of all spiritual evolution, and is in heaven, in the fullest and most immediate presence of God and the most intimate communion with him. And the fact that ' the man Christ Jesus ' has attained this fullness of life is the pledge of our hope that we too may attain it. This heavenly life is true life: being spiritual, it is not less real but far more real than earthly life: it is the life which we were created to inherit, and it lasts for ever. The heavens and the earth will pass away, but Christ's gospel will never pass away. From the beginning of his life on earth he put himself deliberately

The Spiritual Meaning 13

under human conditions and underwent the experiences of humanity, and to the end he maintained the same unity of nature and outlook with mankind: even his relation to the Father he shares, as man, with other men—'I ascend unto my Father and your Father, and to my God and your God' (*St. John* xx. 17). So his Ascension into heaven makes him the first among many brethren, the firstfruits of the human race. (1 *Cor.* xv. 23.)

This life which Christians hope to share with him hereafter is the fulfilment of the spiritual life of man begun here on earth: it is no new life, but the natural and proper development of that on which we are already entered. It differs from earthly life only in the wider range and added fullness which it there takes on. It is not subject to the checks and limitations which are peculiar to the transient life of 'flesh and blood.' St. Paul, who has a unique claim to have seen some revelation while yet on earth of Christ's glorified body after his Ascension (see *Acts* ix. 3–9), gives us the result of his reflections on that vision in 1 *Cor.* xv.; and while he emphasizes the fact that the life hereafter is one and continuous with our earthly life, he strongly insists upon three features of it, which depend upon its being wholly spiritual—incorruption, glory, and power. (1 *Cor.* xv. 42–44.)

Secondly, Christ's Ascension is the guarantee

14 The Spiritual Meaning

of his universal lordship and priesthood. 'The Ascension was at once an end and a beginning —the close of one dispensation and the dawn of another. It limits and unites the life of Christ and the life of his Church, or rather, to express the same thought differently, the life of Christ in his humiliation and the life of Christ in glory. . . . It is the Ascension that brings him who died and rose again within the reach of every child of man, throughout all the ages and throughout all the earth. It makes that to be universal which was seen to be limited before.'

So writes Bishop Westcott. Christ's special functions of Prophet, Priest, and King, belong to him as man and the captain of men: and during the days of his earthly sojourn they could only be exercised with all the natural limitations of space and time which appertain to human activity on earth. But since his Ascension he has exercised them universally without being subject to those limitations, through his Holy Spirit. So we may truly picture him riding through and through the world, conquering and to conquer; 'to the one a savour from death unto death, to the other a savour from life unto life' (2 *Cor.* ii. 16).

'All things are put under his feet,' writes the late Dr. Scott Holland. 'He is made Lord over all powers of God that can conceivably work for our good. His name supplies the key to their use, his will releases them,

The Spiritual Meaning 15

his mind interprets them, his cross and passion bring them into play, his intercession determines their application. The entire force of divine redemption scattered throughout the world in a thousand manifestations is in his hands to administer; it has its seat in his body, it is taken up into his royalty, and it flows down to us through his sanction, under his benediction, by his word. For he is the sum and consummation of all things, and that for ever, until the whole earth has become his, and all that works against God has been subdued under his supremacy; until the end is come, and the kingdoms of the world are become kingdoms of our God and of his Christ.'

And in particular, his atoning sacrifice is universalized. The life he offered once on the cross, he ever lives to present within the veil. And the same life is presented by the same High Priest on every Christian altar; every Mass gives to his own on earth a share in the great sacrificial worship of heaven. ' Alleluia, thou art here, we ask not how.' Space and time are annihilated in that Eucharistic act: the true Priest and Victim is a present reality.

Such, then, is something of what we mean by belief in the Ascension. Allegorize it and spiritualize it as we will, it remains, nevertheless, the central hope of all the prophets and kings, of all the sighs and tears, of the older dispensation, as well as of the clearer vision

16 The Spiritual Meaning

and fuller faith of the new. Without the Ascension the Christian faith is an empty husk, an ideal of moral character, a merely intellectual conviction. Even the resurrection of Jesus would have been an event of comparatively small significance, if it had been no more than a return to life on earth for a shorter or a longer space of time. Nor indeed would the Ascension itself have been anything, had it been only an assumption, or the apotheosis of some hero divinity. It is more than that; more than any event, more than any process. It is one of the great facts of the spiritual order. As such it can never be a mere piece of embroidery on the Christian religion, nor a mere chapter put in to form a fitting conclusion to its story: it is nothing less than the mainspring of its activity, the heart and centre of its enthusiasm and its hope. Christianity without the Ascension will end where all religions have ended, which have tried to find in the earthly life of our Lord, or of some other person, enough to satisfy the highest needs of men. Man's heart is meant for God, and for heaven: his treasure, if on earth, will fail him. ' Even though we have known Christ after the flesh, yet now we know him so no more ' (2 *Cor.* v. 16). But to those who believe in the Ascension, that treasure is imperishable, because it is in heaven, ' where Christ is, seated on the right hand of God ' (*Coloss.* iii. 1).

THE CONGRESS BOOKS: No. 8

THE
HOLY GHOST

G. C. JOYCE, D.D.
*Canon of St. Asaph, late
Principal of St. David's
College, Lampeter*

LONDON
THE SOCIETY OF
SS. PETER & PAUL
32 George St., Hanover Sq., W. 1, *and
The Abbey House, Westminster, S.W.* 1

The Holy Ghost

'I BELIEVE in the Holy Ghost.' 'I believe in the Holy Ghost, the Lord, and giver of life, who proceedeth from the Father and the Son, who with the Father and the Son together is worshipped and glorified, who spake by the prophets.' 'The Father is God, the Son is God: and the Holy Ghost is God. . . . The Holy Ghost is of the Father and of the Son: neither made, nor created, nor begotten, but proceeding.' With these clauses from the three creeds of the Church we are quite familiar. Yet the truth conveyed in the familiar words is larger than the mind of man can grasp, and higher than the mind of man can reach. The doctrine of the Holy Ghost is one of the central and basic mysteries of the Christian faith. We shall do well if from time to time we come back to the study of it. We must needs ask the Holy Spirit himself to give us fresh light on the mystery of his own nature, and of his work upon the world and in our hearts.

The Christian doctrine of the Holy Ghost was not suddenly introduced into the world,

The Spirit of God

ready made, finished and complete. During countless centuries, whilst man was painfully climbing up the first difficult steps of his upward progress, he was learning some elementary lessons about the Spirit of God. Even in the most primitive forms of religion there appear certain notions about God, which, however mixed with error, contain some precious elements of truth. Whatever truth there was, was due to the self-revelation of himself by the Holy Ghost, whose function it is always to bring light.

Led by the Spirit man began dimly to grope after some explanation of the world in which he found himself struggling for his existence. It is a remarkable fact that however far back we may go in the history of man we never find him to have been a materialist. The denial of any spiritual existence is not man's first thought. It is a miserable confusion into which he has falsely argued himself. Nor have these perverted reasonings appealed to him in his early stages. For the most part they have been the product of irreligious civilizations.

Of course men's first ideas about the Spirit of God were exceedingly crude. Their thoughts about the material world were equally childish. It appears that they imagined the power of God to reside in certain objects much as we now think of the electricity in the live wire. To come near to such an object in which was the Spirit of God seemed to them to be dan-

4   The Spirit of God

gerous in the extreme. Traces of this very primitive notion may be found lingering even in the Old Testament. Thus Uzzah is struck dead because unwarily he touches the ark of God (2 *Sam.* vi. 6). It is easy to criticize; but it is more important to observe how from the earliest times men were conscious of the near presence of some mighty spiritual power.

The progress of religion may be traced in the slow correction of human thought about the indwelling Spirit. The history of this development is set before us in the Old Testament. There we may see how the inspired teachers of the people of God were led to take higher and higher views of the nature of the Spirit, and of his connexion with the spirit of man. It was a marked advance when it was understood that the Spirit of God resided rather in man than in any material thing. Samson achieves his feats of strength because the Spirit of God is in him. When the Spirit of God comes upon Saul he falls into a kind of frenzy. The idea is less mechanical than that of the residence of the Spirit of God in stone or tree, but it is still very far from the truth as it became known to the great prophets of Israel.

To them it was shown that the spirit of man can only become the dwelling-place of the Spirit of God provided that there be a moral purification of man's nature. 'Thus saith the high and lofty one that inhabiteth

The Spirit of God

eternity, whose name is Holy; I dwell in the high and holy place, with him also that is of a contrite and humble spirit ' (*Isai.* lvii. 15). More especially did the prophets look forward to a glorious future when the Messianic King should rule in peace and righteousness by reason of the indwelling presence of the Spirit. ' The Spirit of the Lord shall rest upon him, the spirit of wisdom and understanding, the spirit of counsel and might, the spirit of knowledge and of the fear of the Lord ' (*Isai.* xi. 2). Occasionally, but seldom, the epithet ' holy ' is applied to the Spirit. ' Take not thy holy Spirit from me ' (*Psal.* li. 11). Generally speaking, the Old Testament writers think of the Spirit of God as of his power and influence manifesting itself in the glories of nature, in the movements of history, and in the personal life of man. Apart from this preparation of the ground the further revelations about the nature and work of the Spirit that came through the incarnation of our Lord would have been unintelligible and inaccessible. Only because men had learnt the elements of the truth in previous generations were they able to receive and welcome the new truth as it was set before them in Jesus Christ.

6   The Spirit in the Gospel

GOD'S revelation of himself is conveyed to man primarily through events which he brings to pass. The true meaning of the events is explained in the words of inspired teachers and writers. Remembering this principle we shall in the first instance look to the events of our Lord's life for further knowledge of the Holy Ghost. That life was from the first to the last in all its activities and in all its experiences controlled by the Holy Ghost. It is the action of the Holy Ghost which initiates the human life of our Lord. 'Conceived by the Holy Ghost': this is the concise statement of the creed.

It would be impossible to enter upon the many difficult points of controversial criticism that arise in connexion with the Virgin Birth. Our knowledge of the fact is based upon the evidence of only two writers, the authors of the first and third gospels. Possibly there are allusions to it in other books of the New Testament, but they are not so unmistakably clear as to be beyond dispute. On the other hand the narratives of the Birth in *St. Matthew* and *St. Luke* are independent of one another. They differ in certain details and are not altogether easy to harmonize. Yet they converge in their testimony to the Virgin Birth at Bethlehem. The various attempts made to account for the origin of the story, as due to the influence of heathen mythology, or to

The Spirit in the Gospel

a misinterpretation of the prophecy in *Isaiah*, have broken down. Those to whom the doctrine of the Incarnation appears to be the only possible key to the spiritual history of the world, cannot but recognize the fitness of the Virgin Birth. That the human nature through which the Son of God was to effect the redemption of mankind, breaking the terrible entail of sin and introducing a new principle of spiritual life into the race, should have been thus assumed, is altogether appropriate. Here was a new creation in which as in the creation of the natural world the Holy Spirit of God was at work.

The Baptism marks a crisis of first rate importance in the life of our Lord. It was a moment of transition. Till now he had dwelt apart in the retirement of the village home at Nazareth. Henceforth he would gather around him the sick and the sorrowful, bringing healing and comfort. He would preach the gospel of the near approach of the kingdom of God. To know what passed in the mind of our Lord may well be beyond our power. We can but venture to conjecture with all possible caution and with deepest reverence. Devout students have supposed that through the vision and the voice from heaven there came to our Lord a fuller consciousness of his Messianic destiny and mission. In order to be rendered equal to the accomplishment of the great task his human nature

8 The Spirit in the Gospel

was then anointed with the Holy Ghost. In the strength thus given, and following the Holy Spirit's guidance, he went forth into the wilderness to meet the Tempter and to overcome him. From the same source came the power with which he wrought his miracles of mercy. Under the same guidance he trod the road which led to Calvary, through the eternal Spirit offering himself without spot to God (*Hebr.* ix. 14).

Among the recorded words of our Lord there are many that throw light upon the mystery of the Person and work of the Holy Spirit. Of these none have more endeared themselves to the hearts of his followers than the discourses in the Fourth Gospel. There we find the promise of the Paraclete. In our English version the word is rendered 'Comforter.' He is indeed the Comforter who brings consolation and strength. Yet there are reasons for thinking that a more accurate rendering would be the 'Advocate,' who stands by the side of men to defend and protect them against the accusations and slanders of their enemy.

His coming could not be before the departure of our Lord. ' If I go not away, the Comforter will not come unto you ' (*St. John* xvi. 7). When this condition of departure had been satisfied then the Comforter should come, and should bring with him the very presence which for a time appeared to be withdrawn. This

The Spirit in the Gospel

same Comforter should be the guide and instructor of the disciples, reminding them of all that the Master had said, and revealing therein meanings which hitherto had been hidden from their eyes.

A very remarkable verse indicates the effect which the presence of the Comforter should produce upon the world. 'He, when he is come, will convict the world in respect of sin, of righteousness, and of judgement' (*St. John* xvi. 8). Lack of conviction about the first principles of the spiritual realm shuts off the possibility of spiritual progress. If men are to open their hearts to higher influences they must begin by believing in the fact of sin, in the possibility of righteousness, and in the absolute opposition of the one to the other. Men cannot reach these convictions through the mere exercise of their own reasoning powers. Whether they are conscious of it or not, they owe them to the operation of the Holy Ghost within the heart.

Upon his disciples after the Resurrection our Lord solemnly bestows the gift of the Holy Ghost. 'Receive the Holy Ghost: whose soever sins ye forgive, they are forgiven unto them ; whose soever sins ye retain, they are retained' (*St. John* xx. 23). The author of the first gospel tells us that in his last commission our Lord ordained Baptism in the threefold name of Father, Son, and Holy Ghost. (*St. Matt.* xxviii. 19.)

10 The Spirit in the Church

THE history of the primitive Church is nothing else than the record of the new and astonishing experiences caused by the indwelling presence of the Holy Ghost. The ardently expected fulfilment of the promise came on the day of Pentecost. The Church came into being; and the characteristic note of the Church was and is her relation to the Spirit. She is the Spirit-bearing body, in which and through which the Spirit works. In those early years there were certain outward manifestations by which the advent of the Spirit was notified. Prominent among these evidences was the gift of tongues. The intensity of joy and exultation caused by the inflow of the Spirit into the heart vented itself in a burst of ecstatic utterance. There was sound, modulated-like speech, but usually unintelligible to others than the speakers themselves. Other gifts there were, such as the ability to prophesy, to heal diseases, and to work miracles. The common characteristic of all of them was a marvellous increase of the powers of human nature. Men felt themselves to be, as indeed they were, supernaturally endowed. In the midst of the excitement so caused they needed to be reminded that better than any miraculous gifts was the way of charity. The Spirit's power was best displayed in the production of his fruit of love and joy and peace.

The Spirit in the Church

Out of the Christian experience of the Spirit there arose a Christian theology of the Spirit. It was a slow growth. The first generations of Christians were content to live in the Spirit. They neither desired nor needed to find a precise formula for the expression of their thought. Reluctantly, and only in opposition to the spread of error, did the Church undertake the difficult and dangerous task of definition. In carrying out this duty her one object was to be true to the facts of her spiritual experience. Accordingly it is not in the New Testament, but in the writings of the Christian Fathers, that we shall look for an ordered and systematic statement of the Christian faith about the Holy Ghost. It is an intricate and long story, nor can we do more than try to bring out one or two of the main points.

In the fourth century the great issue was clearly raised. Is the Holy Ghost truly God? There were some who held the Holy Ghost to be no more than a name for an impersonal influence proceeding from the divine being, or just an aspect of God in his dealings with men. There were others who held that the Holy Ghost was a created being, a kind of superior angel. To neither of these perverted theories would the Church yield her assent.

Her great teachers, St. Athanasius, St. Basil, St. Gregory of Nazianzus, and St. Gregory of Nyssa, devoted themselves to the

12 The Spirit in the Church

task of finding words in which to set forth the truth. To them the Godhead of the Holy Ghost is beyond dispute. He is inseparable from the Father and the Son, associated with them in glory and worship. Although for the sake of convenience we may properly speak of the second and third Persons of the Trinity, this must not be understood to mean that there is any 'second' or 'third' in God. There is no subordination. And in God there is no separate action on the part of the three Persons. The Father does nothing by himself in which the Son is not joined with him, nor does the Son work apart from the Spirit. All divine action upon the creature takes its origin from the Father, passes through the Son, and is completed in the Holy Spirit.

While it was held to be part of the Catholic faith that the three Persons were in glory equal and in majesty coeternal, it was also taught that each Person was distinctively himself. It is proper to the Father to be made of none, to the Son to be begotten, to the Holy Ghost to proceed. So far there is agreement between the Church of the East and the Church of the West. It is a matter of profound sorrow that in their statement of belief about the procession of the Holy Spirit a divergence has arisen. The Western Church has inserted into the common creed of Christendom the words 'and the Son,' adding them to the clause 'proceeding from the

Works of the Spirit 13

Father.' Against this addition the Eastern Church protests.

That there is a difference in the form of words used in the East and in the West is undeniable. But in the thought behind the words is real agreement. The West holds no less strongly than the East that there can be only one ultimate source of the divine life and that this source is the Father. The statement that the Spirit proceeds from the Father and the Son does not mean that there are two sources of the Spirit's life, but that the divine life passes from the Father through the Son to the Spirit. The time may not be far distant when mutual explanations shall prove satisfactory, and the long-standing cause of difference between East and West shall be finally removed.

THE works of the one Spirit are manifold indeed. 'Every thought of holiness is his alone.' Among his activities we distinguish some that stand out with especial prominence. 'Inspiration' is one of these. It can only be understood when we refer it to the action of the Holy Spirit upon the mind and heart of the many writers of the books of the Bible. During the last century we have become more aware of the human element

14 Works of the Spirit

in the Bible than were our forefathers. Rigid and mechanical views of inspiration, which reduced the writer to the position of a mere pen in the hand of the Holy Spirit, are no longer maintained. We believe that the effect of the action of the Spirit upon prophet and psalmist and historian, was to elevate and enlighten their power of spiritual vision. They remained men of their time and of their country. But thus enlightened they were empowered to give utterance to truths transcending the limitations of time and of place. The Bible took roughly a thousand years to write, and it is impossible to compute the number of its contributors. Yet its unity is unmistakable. Its various parts dovetail into one system of thought. Thus it affords manifest evidence of its derivation from the one Spirit of God. And the same is true of all inspiration down to the present day. To the guidance of the Holy Spirit alone can we ascribe the revelation of truth by the teacher, the moral insight of the prophet, and the mystical union of the saint with God in contemplative prayer.

Frequently objections have been raised to the sacramental system of the Church on the ground that sacraments partake of the nature of magic. The best way to deal with these criticisms is to point to the intimate connexion between the doctrine of sacraments and the doctrine of the Holy Ghost. The

Works of the Spirit 15

sacraments are the covenanted means by which the virtue and grace of the death and resurrection of Jesus Christ are bestowed upon the souls of men : and the efficacy of those sacraments is due wholly to the action of his Spirit. It is the Holy Spirit who in Baptism, supplemented with the laying on of hands in Confirmation, confers the gift of the new life, together with the powers required for its exercise. In the early baptismal services the Holy Spirit is invoked at more than one point. 'King and Lord of all things, look upon these waters and fill them with the Holy Spirit.' Likewise early forms of ordination are explicit in their recognition of the action of the Spirit in conferring Orders.

It is of especial interest to notice the invocation of the Holy Ghost in the Eucharist, technically called the *epiklesis*. This invocation occurs in the earliest known Consecration Prayer. In the East it became the current view that the consecration of the elements was thereby effected. In the West a different opinion prevailed. Yet the practice of the invocation of the Holy Spirit was widespread in the West also. By many it is earnestly desired that it should be introduced into our own Liturgy : because it gives expression to the truth that it is the Holy Spirit, acting in the name of Christ that sent him, who really makes the bread and the wine become the body and the blood of our Saviour.

16 Works of the Spirit

To the action of the Holy Spirit within the individual heart is due every good desire, every resistance to temptation, and every good work. Not only is it he who illuminates the mind, it is also he who warms the heart with love. Man is only truly alive when he is putting into action powers that find their expression in love, joy, peace, longsuffering, gentleness, goodness, faith, meekness, self-control. For these are the fruit of the Spirit who is the giver of life. To dwell on the high doctrine of the Holy Ghost as taught by the Catholic Church is to arouse within ourselves the longing for a more abundant spiritual life. O God, make clean our hearts within us : and take not thy Holy Spirit from us.

THE CONGRESS BOOKS: No. 9

MIRACLES

ARTHUR CHANDLER, D.D.,
Late Bishop of
Bloemfontein ::

LONDON
THE SOCIETY OF
SS. PETER & PAUL
32 *George St., Hanover Sq., W.* 1, *and*
The Abbey House, Westminster, S.W. 1

Miracles

IF we are to approach the question of Miracles, and in particular the miracles of Jesus Christ, satisfactorily, we should bear in mind two important facts with regard to the universe as we know it. In the first place, the universe of our knowledge and experience is one and continuous throughout, with no abrupt or violent breaks to divide it up into alien and hostile compartments. And, secondly, within this unity there is progress and variety; the universe is not all on one uniform level, but rather resembles a ladder of ascending steps; it is a whole embracing parts which are different from each other, and must be differently explained and interpreted.

The first principle, that of the unity and continuity of truth, lies at the root of all inquiry and research. It assures us that, however different the various departments of truth may be, they are all somehow united and interconnected, just as the differently shaped and coloured bits of wood fit together ultimately in a jigsaw puzzle. If there were nothing but difference, no underlying unity of scheme and

The Category of Mechanism 3

purpose, science and inquiry would be impracticable, or could only consist in registering variety without being able to reduce it to law and order.

And the second principle, that of diversity within the unity, a diversity of grades and aspects and degrees of reality, is necessary if we are to understand the world in the manifold variety of its messages and its significance.

Both these principles will prove to be of the utmost importance as we consider the nature and credibility of miracles. The principle of unity and continuity will teach us to think of miracles not as arbitrary occurrences, different from and exceptions to the course of nature, but rather as special expressions of the same supreme power which expresses itself in all the course of nature ; and the principle of diversity, which prevents us from thinking that everything in the world is on one dead level of uniformity, will save us from dogmatically asserting that the events known as miracles are impossible in one sphere because they are not found in another.

IRST, then, let us take the latter principle, the principle of diversity—the fact that the world of our experience is not all on one level, but is broken up into hills and valleys ; that it consists of various depart-

4 The Category of Mechanism

ments of fact which, being different, must be explained from different points of view; that the doors admitting us to these various departments must be opened by different keys. These keys, or points of view, are called 'categories.' A category is a keyword, a typical or generic conception which expresses shortly the sort or class of experience we are dealing with, and the point of view from which we must look at it.

The great majority of our mistakes in our view of the universe spring from a wrong application of categories; from our trying to open a door with a key which does not fit that particular lock.

The lowest step on the ladder, the lowest stage in the world of truth, is the sphere of inorganic things, dealt with in the shape of atoms and molecules by chemistry, and under the name of matter and force by physics. And the characteristic of these things is that they are made up of parts which are external to each other and independent of each other, acting on each other in accordance with mathematical laws of causation. Throughout this whole department of fact, the category or key-word which sums it up and expresses it is *mechanism;* and we must understand what mechanism and mechanical really mean. Things that can be mechanically explained are dead things, external to, and independent of each other, and regulated by chemical and physical laws of causation.

Organism and Personality 5

If we look at some great machine, like the machinery which propels a steamer, we see that all the parts, the cogs and wheels and pistons, are indeed marvellously adapted to each other; but this adaptation is not a self-adaptation; it has been impressed upon them from outside, and comes from the mind of the designer or engineer. The various parts of the machine have no interest in each other, or in the whole of which they are parts, or in the object for which the whole has been made; in themselves they are absolutely indifferent to each other; they co-operate not by any act of their own, but by an act from without, over which they have no control.

The mechanical sphere, then, is a sphere of things existing alongside of each other in space, acting and re-acting on each other unconsciously in accordance with necessary law.

Then we rise to a higher sphere, the department of living things, whether vegetable or animal. And here the leading characteristic is that we are not dealing now with parts which are external to and independent of each other, but with parts that are essentially and inherently related to each other and to the whole which comprises them. The parts are, of their own nature, associated together to build up the whole, are governed and regulated by the whole, and subserve the good of the whole. The good of the animal, its life and self-preservation, is the end which governs and directs the action

6   Organism and Personality

of all the limbs and nerves and muscles; and this end or purpose pervades the parts; it is inherent in them, instead of being imposed upon them from outside, as in the case of a mechanism. The all-pervasive life of the animal, struggling to maintain itself, is the whole which uses the action of the parts, and to which the parts in their turn minister.

The key-word of this department is, then, *organism*, or a living relationship of part and whole. But it cost a long struggle before scientific men consented to recognize that we have here a fresh department of fact, which must be looked at from a fresh point of view, and calls for a fresh category to interpret it. A stubborn attempt was made to maintain that a living organism can be explained in the same way as a dead mechanism. The persistence of this attempt, and its utter failure, can be studied in a very interesting little book called 'Mechanism, Life, and Personality,' by Dr. Haldane (Murray).

A third department is reached when we come to the action and life of human beings. Here, in place of the blind striving of an organism to maintain its life in the face of its environment, we have action based on perception and volition (or will); in other words, free conscious action. The difference between such action and that of an animal or vegetable organism is so great as to demand a fresh point of view from which to consider it, a

Organism and Personality

fresh category or key-word to express it. Such a point of view, or key-word, is found in the term *personality*. But, just as desperate efforts were made to explain organic life from the standpoint of mechanics, so here similar efforts have been made to explain personal life from the point of view of an organism. And just as the sciences of chemistry and physics were invoked to explain organic life, so here physiology and biology (sciences of organic life) are asked to explain the whole sphere of personal human action.

But such an attempt is as desperate as the other. The category of organic life is simply misplaced when made the key-word of human thought and endeavour. Of course we may, for special purposes, choose to look at a man merely from the standpoint of his animal nature. But to treat him in such a way is to take an abstract, one-sided, fragmentary point of view ; if we are to look at him as a whole, and especially if we are to consider the qualities which mark him off from other animals, we must maintain that human knowledge and human volition are fresh facts, which demand a fresh key to interpret them.

Here, then, we have clear instances of diversity and variety, of ascending grades and different levels, which must be recognized within the unity of experience ; and have seen the futility of trying to explain the higher grades by categories which belong to the lower.

8 When God had become Man

THEN, further, we come face to face with the life and actions of Jesus Christ ; and as we read, with an open mind, the documents in which they are recorded, our impression is that we are there confronted with one who moves and lives on a different level to the rest of mankind ; on a level so different as to make it natural that many of his actions should be of a sort that are impossible for ourselves. This was certainly the feeling which found expression again and again from the lips of bystanders : ' Rabbi, thou art the Son of God ; thou art the King of Israel ' ; ' My Lord and my God ' ; ' Thou art the Christ, the Son of the living God.' In other words, a fresh category, a new key-word, seems to be required in order to open and explain this fresh department of fact : the category or key-word of *God-incarnate*.

But here again the old tendency is manifested to level down the higher stages of truth, and explain the loftiest facts of experience in terms of those below. It is this philosophical prejudice, rather than any doubt as to the character of the documents, which causes people to reject the record of his miracles. They are determined not to recognize here a higher level of existence, and not to place him in a higher grade of being than their own. They are prepared to accept in the case of Christ any action of the sort that they can

When God had become Man 9

themselves perform, but no others. Thus 'Liberal Protestants' (sometimes popularly called Modernists) accept him as a great teacher, who had a profound experience of God's Fatherhood and a temperament acutely sensitive to spiritual values; while 'Modernists' regard him as an other-worldly prophet, inspired by a conviction of the approaching end of this world and of his own mission to inaugurate a new one. He is credited with possessing all our capacities in the highest development of which purely human capacities are susceptible; but miracles, such as are narrated in the New Testament, go beyond these capacities, and must therefore be rejected.

Here, then, we have a crowning instance of the tendency which we have so often met with —the fallacy of denying diversity and craving for uniformity; the fallacy of trying to unlock different doors with one key, and to level down all ascending grades and varieties which we find within the unity of truth.

To accept the Incarnation in any real and distinctive sense and to reject Christ's miracles seems quite unreasonable. The Incarnation means that a new, divine power came into the world at a certain time; and when a new power has emerged it is natural to expect that it may manifest itself in new ways. We do not deny that a dog can grow and move itself because a flint can do neither. The dog represents a new power, accompanied by a new mode of action.

We do not deny that a man is able to talk or to choose between right and wrong because a dog can do neither. And we shall not deny that Christ could multiply loaves or walk on the sea or raise the dead because these things are beyond our power. Each new fact manifests itself in new ways; each higher power, as it comes forth, exercises higher modes of action, which are natural and normal for it, however abnormal or miraculous they might be in a lower sphere. Our Lord's ' mighty works ' are miracles from our point of view, while being at the same time natural and normal exhibitions of a power present in him, though not in us.

Last in the scale of being, we rise from God-incarnate to *God as such*—God in his eternal and essential nature, in which he is, among other things, the creator and ruler of the universe. In him everything in the world finds its ultimate explanation and attains its true reality. The higher we ascend, the more do things come together and get explained; in God the end and purpose of them all is reached; in technical language, they are ' teleologically determined ' in reference to him. So, if God is the ultimate and all-comprehensive explanation and sovereign ruler of the whole, the world is from beginning to end a spiritual world, a world made, permeated, indwelt, and ruled by God. The normal processes of ' nature ' are not independent of him, but are just the normal expression of his will; and he is free

God and Nature

to alter the mode in which his will is expressed if it seems good to him to do so; what we call miracles will then come about; but both modes of action, the normal and the abnormal, express one and the same spiritual will of God, and illustrate at once the power, the intelligence, and the freedom with which that will is exercised.

So miracles are not only 'natural' in the case of Christ, because of the special powers belonging to him as God-incarnate, but are further natural as operations of God the creator and sustainer of a universe which is stamped throughout with his own spiritual nature, and subject at every point to his spiritual will. Thus it is not only in the actions of Christ that miracles are to be regarded as credible and appropriate; but both before and after his life on earth the supreme spiritual will of God may deal as he pleases with the processes of the world which he made, and which he ever guides and controls.

It is extraordinary what a limited and unworthy view people generally take of the divine action; and how fond they are of illustrating it from the movements of the sun and stars. No doubt there is something calm and majestic in the action of these bodies; but, after all, such movement is the movement of dead matter, and far lower in kind than the growth of a cabbage or the wriggling of a tadpole—where at any rate life is present. If we are to think

12 All Nature one World

worthily of God, we must think of him in the light of the highest that we know, in the light of free personal life, not of dead mechanical movement. To condemn miracles on the ground that they contradict a mechanical regularity of natural process is to degrade God to a far lower level than our own, and to argue that he can only act by blind necessary law, whilst our own acts proceed from motives and ideals of free personal life, and are acts which we are free to alter or modify in view of any special need or crisis that arises. A very signal example this of the misuse of the category of mechanism![1]

ECONDLY, we have to consider the principle of unity and continuity. Scientific men have been shy about recognizing in the universe the principle of diversity, which we have hitherto been discussing, through a nervous dread of seeming to leave 'gaps' in the system of nature, or to accept 'arbitrary interventions' of a divine power, whereby laws would be upset and disorder introduced. But such fears are groundless; the universe is one; there is continuity underlying all the divisions and stages of fact from

[1] For further treatment of this theme I may be allowed to refer to my book *Scala Mundi* (Methuen).

All Nature one World 13

the lowest to the highest ; and this continuity is a far higher and more scientific principle than blank uniformity. In the midst of diversity it preserves the unity of the whole. For instance, the chemical and physical laws which govern the mechanical sphere of inorganic matter continue to operate, in a subordinate function, when taken up into the higher sphere of organic life ; whilst the laws of organic life still act, though no longer supreme, in the case of human action ; and the conditions of human nature are found, though governed and transcended by a higher power, in the case of Christ ; and the power and will of God the creator, with whom Christ is one, form the uniting and permeating principle of the whole.

Unity and continuity exist throughout ; but it is a unity in diversity, a continuity of ascending grades. And this continuity is seen in the fact that it is possible to look at the higher in the light of the lower. In each stage, if we deliberately make abstraction of the features characteristic of it, we can look at its objects as though they belonged to the grade below. Thus, if we like, we can look at animals simply in the light of the chemical and physical laws which govern the sphere of dead matter ; in other words, we can, if we choose, treat animals as mechanisms. By doing so we leave out, of course, just that which is the characteristic feature of animals ; but the mechanical substructure is nevertheless truly taken up into the organic sphere; continuity is preserved; and we can, if we like, fix our attention on the lower and neglect the higher fact.

So, again, we can, if we wish, look at man simply as an animal, from the point of view of the laws which control the nervous system of all animals alike. We can talk of him as though there were nothing in him but sensory nerves with motor discharges, and a complicated system of arteries and muscles. Here, again, we are leaving out the characteristic feature, his personality, or capacity of conscious and volitional action; but the animal bodily structure is in fact taken up into this sphere of personal life, and we can, if we choose, look at it exclusively, to the neglect of consciousness and freedom.

So, too, we can look at Christ, if we choose to do so, in the light of ordinary human personality, as being endowed with our ordinary capacities of knowledge and action, and with nothing beyond. Here, again, we are leaving out the characteristic feature, the category of God-incarnate, which alone explains or interprets him; but it is true that the human nature is in fact taken up into him, and, if we choose, we can fix our attention exclusively on that. And, lastly, we can look at God pantheistically, as though he were identical with the life and structure of the universe, and had no existence above or beyond it. We could

What Miracle Means

only do so by ignoring the fact of primary importance, that he is the creator and master of the universe; but it is true that he pervades the universe and that the universe is explained and united in him; and therefore we can, if we like, identify his action with the working of the normal processes—and even the lowest, mechanical processes—of his universe.

There is, then, an unbroken continuity underlying and connecting together all the ascending phases of fact; the diversity which we see in the universe means not confusion, but orderly progress and advance. Each successive stage takes up and modifies the material of the stage below; and at each higher stage a new power is manifested, producing results which are 'natural' at that stage, but would be abnormal or impossible in the sphere below. Thus, it is natural for a cabbage, which has organic life, to grow and expand in a way which would be impossible in the case of a stone or a star. It is natural for a man, who has conscious personal life, to form a system of knowledge and a scheme of conduct which would be impossible in an animal or a plant. It was natural for our Lord, who had the powers of God-incarnate, to act in a way which would be impossible for mere men. It is natural for almighty God, who is the creator and ruler of the world, to regulate and control its processes and guide its destinies, with a power that belongs to him alone.

16 What Miracle Means

The term 'miracle' is generally confined to cases where the laws or processes of the lower spheres are modified by the exercise of a divine power, as in the two latter instances just given. In this case a miracle might be defined as *the production of special results, for special purposes, by the one spiritual power which is always ruling all the departments of the universe;* or as *a modification of normal sequences of nature by the one spiritual power which governs all things.*

The main principle to insist on is, that a miracle is not to be regarded as an 'exception to a law of nature' (which is a ridiculous and impossible idea), but as a free and orderly operation of a divine power which is itself present and at work at every stage and in every phase of the laws or processes of nature. We shall not expect miracles to be frequent, and we shall not accept them unless they are adequately attested. The normal processes of the universe must be taken to represent God's normal will. But when some great spiritual issue is at stake, like the supreme issue of man's redemption, miracles may well be the simplest and most effective way of dealing with it; and the fact that the power which is at work in the normal processes of nature is still a spiritual power will show that such exceptional action is itself normal and appropriate.

THE CONGRESS BOOKS: No. 10
A SIMPLE LIFE
OF OUR LORD

LEONARD PRESTIGE, B.D.
*Rector of Upper Heyford, Oxon.,
Examining Chaplain to the Bishop of
Oxford, late Fellow of New College*

LONDON
THE SOCIETY OF
SS. PETER & PAUL
32 *George St., Hanover Sq., W.* 1, *and
The Abbey House, Westminster, S.W.* 1

A Simple Life of Our Lord

STRICTLY speaking, the life of our Lord never began and will never end. He is God, from everlasting to everlasting. That is one of the two great facts which St. John teaches in the first few verses of his gospel. It is true that our Lord's friends in Palestine when they first saw him, and indeed most of those who never came to have more than a passing and casual acquaintance with him, did not think of him as God; though probably no one who ever met him thought of him as anything but a very exceptional and highly gifted person. But those who did come to know him intimately were slowly forced to the conclusion, from which they never afterwards swerved, that any statement and any belief which could rightly be applied to God could be applied with equal truth to Jesus Christ; that whatever God was, Christ was also. God and Christ are simply different expressions of the same reality.

The other great fact taught in the prologue of St. John's gospel is that this divine person, Jesus Christ, possessed all the attributes of a

Christ's Birth

genuine human being. He was God clothed in humanity, born in the flesh, and become one of us men. He was God who had put himself into the position and circumstances in which he could think, feel, act, and live in the same way as men think, feel, act, and live. That is what we imply by the word incarnation, which really means 'being put into flesh,' or 'being put into human nature.' There was never any doubt among those who knew Christ about his being genuinely human. Any and every positive element, physical, mental, and moral, which can be said to contribute to the authentic make-up of mankind, was to be found fully and plainly in the composition of Jesus of Nazareth.

These two facts taken together yield the only satisfactory key to the understanding of the earthly life and career of Jesus, which is what we are now about to study.

He was born at a time when his nation, the Jews, after many changes of fortune, had finally lost the political independence which counted for so much in their religious mind and feelings, and had become an outlying and unimportant dependency of the Roman Empire. They longed for deliverance: indeed for centuries they had been led to expect the appearance of some sort of deliverer from their varied and almost continuous tribulations. Sometimes they looked for the rising of a great Messianic leader from among themselves; sometimes they hoped that a celestial Messiah would descend with miraculous powers from heaven; sometimes they thought that God himself would intervene in person to save them. As it turned out, all these different lines of expectation were fulfilled, but in such a way as none of our Lord's countrymen had ever dreamed.

What actually happened (so the gospels tell us, and it is certainly credible enough, if God exists at all) was this. God did intervene in person. As parallel rays of light can be focused and, as it were, localized in one spot, so Christ, the everlasting Word and Son, assumed a local and physical presence in the womb of blessed Mary, a Jewish virgin, his chosen vessel of grace. He caused his true human body to grow there, by the same mysterious processes as determine the growth of any ordinary child conceived from human seed; and in due course of time, on the first Christmas Day, was born in the stable of an overcrowded inn at Bethlehem, in Judaea. (*St. Luke* i. 1–ii. 38.)

His mother had been betrothed, before the Incarnation, to a man named Joseph, of the family of David, whose trade (according to the Jewish custom that men should be trained to earn a living by manual work) was that of a carpenter. When the facts were revealed to him he had accepted the situation as occasioned by the purpose and deed of God, and had taken Mary and her unborn child under his protec-

Christ's Birth

tion, as her nominal husband. This, and the fact that our Lord was born away from home, secured the holy family against vulgar scandal. It was thus with Joseph as protector that the infant Jesus was visited by the shepherds, worshipped by wise men from the East (representatives in the divine providence of the whole Gentile world), and guarded from the jealous blood-lust of the ferocious and decrepit Herod 'the Great,' Rome's puppet king. Apparently the holy family settled for a time at Bethlehem, which was indeed the purpose of the census regulation requiring their presence there at all. But within two years of his birth they were forced to fly from Herod's dominions, when the male babies of the village of Bethlehem were massacred; and for a time took refuge in Egypt, which had been for centuries the natural exile of fugitive Jews. As soon as Herod's death (4 B.C.) was known, Joseph and his charges returned, to find the old king's dominions divided between his sons; and since Herod Archelaus, who inherited Judaea, equalled his father in ferocity, Joseph prudently avoided Bethlehem and withdrew to Nazareth in the hills of Galilee, where Mary's home had been before the birth of Christ. (*St. Matt.* i. and ii.)

Only one further incident do we know of in the course of our Lord's childhood. When he was twelve years old, possibly on the occasion of the next in the recurring cycle of

Roman censuses, he was taken to the feast of Passover at Jerusalem; and when the learned doctors sat to instruct the people he attracted notice by the unusual development of his intelligence, and somewhat startled his mother by his clear expression, even at that early age, of a sense of divine mission. Beyond this, we know of him only as the perfect son in the truly ideal home. (*St. Luke* ii. 39–52.)

This silence and privacy is significant of the policy which all through his life our Lord consistently maintained.

He did not come to preach a gospel of human goodness and holiness with which men were not to be given the opportunity of making themselves fully and practically acquainted; and he required people to recognize and to acknowledge both his goodness and his deity by their own natural qualities and for their own intrinsic value. That is why, later on, he so often refused to work a sign. He would be accepted, if at all, only because of his real and undeniable worth, from the inward conviction of the heart.

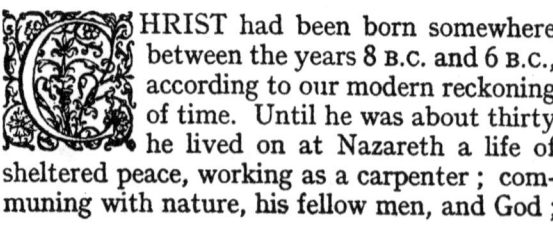

CHRIST had been born somewhere between the years 8 B.C. and 6 B.C., according to our modern reckoning of time. Until he was about thirty he lived on at Nazareth a life of sheltered peace, working as a carpenter; communing with nature, his fellow men, and God;

Christ's Manhood

and learning to love and understand life in a way that only a good man could, and to a degree that no other man has ever attained. Then a new religious movement, which seems to have been quietly gathering force for years, was brought to a head, probably in the year A.D. 26, by our Lord's kinsman John, later called the Baptist.

For centuries no successor had appeared in Jewry to the interrupted line of the Old Testament prophets. Suddenly John from his desert hermitage took up their mantle, and called upon his countrymen to repent of their moral failings, for the long-expected Messiah was at hand. Gathering a band of disciples round him, he preached to the crowds which flocked to him from all classes of society, and as a sign or symbol of their repentance caused those whom his preaching had converted to be washed or 'baptized' in the river Jordan.

John's mission touched and kindled all that was vital in Jewish religion; and among those who came to be baptized was Christ. John hesitated to baptize him, recognizing his spiritual superior; but our Lord insisted. For one thing, he thereby undertook the character of representative of all mankind. For Christ himself, and John, the event had a special significance. As our Lord ascended from the river a dove alighted on him. It was a sign that he was pre-eminently anointed by God with the divine Spirit, and fitly expressed the fact that his whole life, while genuinely human, was in fact lived in entire accordance with the will of God, was inspired and dominated and directed by the Holy Spirit. 'Thou art my beloved Son, in thee I am well pleased.' It may have added something to the self-conscious intuition of our Lord: it certainly made John suddenly realize to his own satisfaction that his spotless but retiring kinsman was the very Messiah whom he preached.

Immediately Christ went into retreat in the desert, to learn of God, and to break the power of the temptations which now assailed him. These were closely connected with his mission, and correspond with three conspicuous failings in the Messianic expectations of his Jewish contemporaries. One was that he should aim at satisfying merely physical cravings—the temptation of selfish materialism. The second was that he should make concessions of principle to the spirit of the age, and by acquiring worldly leadership try to lead men on to higher things. This would have meant the lowering of his unearthly ideals, and he rejected it as he had the former temptation. The third was in a way the subtlest. He was driven to Jerusalem, and mounted to the pinnacle of the Temple, where the impulse assailed his tortured spirit to convince men of his claims by throwing himself down, and by a miraculously safe descent

Christ's Manhood

to win the confidence of the people. That was the temptation to use sensational and superficial methods, instead of appealing to the conscience and spiritual perception of mankind. Once and for all he rejected that too : and the devil could do no more. (*St. Luke* iii. 1–23, iv. 1–13.)

After his temptation Christ remained for a time near the Jordan, and gathered round him a little circle of adherents—Andrew and John (later the apostle) from the disciples of John the Baptist, together with Peter, Philip, and Nathanael (who is usually identified with Bartholomew). Then he returned with them to Galilee, and wrought his first miracle by changing water into wine at the marriage feast at Cana. It is worth noticing that this was done in order to strengthen the confidence which his adherents already had begun to form in him : it was not the cause of their faith but his response to it, and only they (and the servants, whose remarks were doubtless dismissed as idle chatter) were aware of what had happened. (*St. John* i. 29–ii. 11.)

Early in the next year (A.D. 27) Christ, with his family, and his followers moved from Nazareth, Bethsaida, or wherever else they had been living previously, and established a joint headquarters at Capernaum, on the north-west corner of the sea of Galilee (*St. John* ii. 12). Thence in the spring he went up to Jerusalem for the passover.

10   Christ's Manhood

On this occasion our Lord took a striking means of proclaiming the true principles of spiritual religion. The Temple courts were the scene of busy ecclesiastical money-making, connected with the provision of sacrifices. Christ drove merchants and merchandise out of the precincts of the Temple with a stern rebuke; and when the Jews asked him the significance of this public act he retorted with a cryptic reply, designed to make them think out the obvious answer for themselves. That was often his way. Yet this manifestation of spiritual claims, so striking and so genuine, elicited only a superficial interest, though our Lord made one secret disciple of importance, Nicodemus, a member of the religious ruling council or Sanhedrin. (*St. John* ii. 13–iii. 15.)

After the feast he kept his followers in Judæa, and caused them to baptize, as John was still doing. Our Lord's own ministry thus began definitely as an extension of the movement initiated by John. But he did not very long continue this work, partly because a fancied rivalry with John was causing scandal, and partly because about this time the profession of public moral reformer became one of extreme danger. Shortly afterwards John was arrested by Herod Antipas (another of the sons of Herod the Great). Jesus, who had no mind to die yet, returned through Samaria to Galilee. (*St. John* iii. 22–iv. 54.)

The Galilean Ministry 11

OUR Lord marked his return, as he had before, by another miracle, again in response to faith. On more than one occasion he seems to have used repetition as a means of practical emphasis, as we shall have further occasion to note. But this time it marked also a definite change and development in his plans, which it will be convenient to consider under three heads.

In the first place, he now adopted a new method of approach: instead of calling the multitudes out into the desert, he carried his preaching of repentance and the kingdom of God into the villages of Galilee. In particular he made full use of opportunities to address the people in their village meeting-houses, or 'synagogues,' in which they met to pray and to be edified on the sabbath: almost every mention of his preaching or working in a synagogue refers to this period of his ministry.

Secondly, he organized his more intimate followers. Previously the friends who had visited Jerusalem with him at the feasts, and had moved to Capernaum to be near him, had continued to pursue their ordinary professions. Many of them were fishermen on the sea of Galilee; and except in the stormy seasons they had not left their work for any great length of time. But now he called upon certain of them to adopt a new profession and become fishers of men; and shortly afterwards, after a whole night of prayer, he selected twelve and constituted them a special body, with the name of apostles. These he sent in couples, on at least two occasions (once with other helpers added), to prepare for his visits or to extend the range of his activity. But in the main they acted as his personal attendants.

Thirdly, his teaching took on a fundamental change of character. Hitherto, like John, he had proclaimed the coming of the kingdom of God as the occasion for a reformation of particular moral failings. But now he began to range over the whole area of religious and moral principles; and in the process of driving men back upon the underlying principles of religion he uttered many startling sayings, and upset many cherished ideas. It is significant that the epoch-making Sermon on the Plain, beginning with the beatitudes, was delivered on the very day on which he had appointed the twelve apostles. And what is more, his teaching sprang direct from the pure well of enlightened conscience and spiritual insight. He did not quote authorities among the rabbis: he did not so much comment upon as re-interpret and extend the sense of Scripture. 'It was said to them of old time, . . . But I say unto you!' This element of personal claim and spiritual certitude, and the graciousness with which it was accompanied, caused not merely remark but astonishment: 'for he taught them as having

The Galilean Ministry

authority, and not as the scribes.' Christ did not think, he knew: and what he knew was obviously right and morally beautiful.

Moreover, he emphasized his personal claims by working a whole series of 'signs.' He always refused to work a miracle to order; but at his own time he worked dozens, chiefly miracles of bodily healing, and usually with a clear moral purpose. He thus supplemented his oral teaching by practical demonstration both of his intention and of his power to put right what was wrong, and to create a radical change in the lives of men. And once at least he made of his capacity to heal the body a test of his authority to forgive sins. He first forgave the sins of the paralytic, and then in answer to objectors proceeded to cure him of his sickness. And though he did not as yet publicly claim to be divine, and even deprecated any tendency to hail him as such, yet the objectors on this occasion rightly murmured that he was assuming a prerogative which belonged to God alone. (*St. Mark* ii. 7.)

This new type of mission caused an enormous impression; crowds flocked to hear Christ, bearing their sick with them. ' We never saw it on this fashion!' To understand the general character of the Galilean ministry we need only read *St. Matt.* iv. 23–ix. 38, in which chapters v.–vii. contain a full summary of Christ's religious teaching, and chapters viii. and ix. a classified collection of his chief miracles. Its immediate effect was that he became at one blow the hero of the peasantry. (*St. Mark* i. 14–iii. 19 ; *St. Luke* iv. 31–vii. 17.)

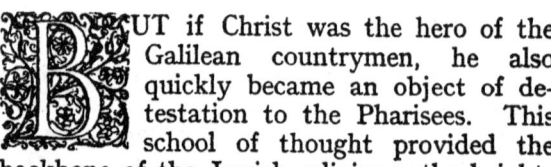UT if Christ was the hero of the Galilean countrymen, he also quickly became an object of detestation to the Pharisees. This school of thought provided the backbone of the Jewish religion ; the heights to which it rose may be measured by Psalm cxix. But it was now steeped in formalism and had lost hold of the realities beneath the outward conventions of religious practice ; so that its suspicions were at once aroused by the vigorous freshness of Christ's life and teaching, and especially by his friendships with social outcasts, his depreciation of formalism in fasting, his disquieting claims to personal authority, and above all his disregard of the elaborated regulations which the Pharisees had developed for observance of the sabbath. (*St. Mark* ii. 1–iii. 6.)

At some time during this year Christ went up to another festival (we do not know which) at Jerusalem, and incurred their hostility by healing on the sabbath. He claimed that, whatever their regulations might be, in giving life and strength he was obviously doing the will of God, and that people's capacity for spiritual perception was in fact being tested or judged by their attitude to his work.

General Failure 15

Conscience and their own Bibles ought to show them this. (*St. John* v.) But their reply was to send spies from Jerusalem to watch him in Galilee; and when these emissaries said that his good works were only able to be done because he was in league with the devil, Christ poured on them the vials of scathing condemnation (*St. Mark* iii. 20–30). The most terrible things he ever said were said of the Pharisees, who valued their own system and theories above spiritual vitality and the facts of life, and only matched their essential worldliness and hypocrisy by their barbarous inhumanity. (Compare *St. Matt.* xxiii.). They never forgave him.

And even John the Baptist wavered. He lay in prison, waiting for death until the murderous influence of Herod Antipas' incestuous concubine should achieve its opportunity. If Jesus were the Christ, why did he not strike, and save his servant? But Christ answered with evidence of the same kind as he set before the rest of the world, and waited his full time. (*St. Luke* vii. 18–35.)

Again, our Lord's success with the multitudes was largely superficial. His own village of Nazareth rejected him. And many of those who followed him were actuated by curiosity, or the desire to gain something from him, like Judas Iscariot. They wanted to be cured, or to hear the popular preacher, or to be entertained with signs, or to see the Pharisees

16 General Failure

routed : they sought 'the meat which perisheth.' And Christ determined deliberately to repel them. He began to avoid the synagogues. And he would only speak publicly in parables, to make them either think for themselves, or abandon the pretence of discipleship—'that seeing they may see, and not perceive; and hearing they may hear, and not understand; lest haply they should turn again, and it should be forgiven them.' (*St. Mark* iv. 1–12; *St. Matt.* xiii.; and compare *St. Luke* ix. 57–62, x. 13–16, xi. 29–36, xiv.–xvi.)

Another consequence was that our Lord took more to the water. He was thronged and pressed by land, and he needed retirement; partly because his work with the crowds was spiritually unprofitable, partly to secure personal leisure and to train his apostles. So we read that he crossed and re-crossed the sea of Galilee. It was at this period that he sent out the two missions of his disciples; of which one object was to break new ground, but another certainly was to let the apostles feel their feet, and to give himself fuller opportunity for prayer, in seclusion from the multitudes.

Then Herod Antipas, who ruled Galilee as well as the desert east of Jordan, began to show an interest in his work; and he crossed the sea to Bethsaida, which was outside Antipas' territory. But the people followed, and found him in the wilderness, where he fed

The Apostles' Faith 17

five thousand of them by a miracle : in consequence of which they tried to make him adopt the political *rôle* which popular enthusiasm expected of the Messiah, and lead them against their Roman rulers. The situation was extremely dangerous. Jesus withdrew alone into the hills, ordering the apostles away by boat, lest they should join in the deluded enterprise of the people ; then at night, to hearten his discouraged band of followers, he overtook their storm-tossed vessel, walking over the water, to their sore amazement. The next day he entered the synagogue at Capernaum (the latest mention of his visiting one), and taught the returning multitudes that his leadership was purely spiritual. This divided them. But the old and dangerous conditions remained : he was once more in Herod's dominions, crowds still pressed, the spies from Jerusalem were active : and Jesus decided to disappear completely, not this time just across the sea of Galilee, but far north into the heathen districts of Tyre and Sidon. (*St. Mark* vi. 7–vii. 24 ; *St. John* vi.)

A YEAR had passed since the first appeal to the villages and synagogues of northern Palestine, and it was now the spring of (probably A.D. 28. The Galilean ministry had secured its paramount object in the gathering of a truly converted remnant, of

18   The Apostles' Faith

which a certain few faithful women and the twelve apostles were the core. Christ's heart now turned almost entirely to them, and especially to the work of training the apostles. By a slow circuitous route he led them gradually south again, keeping in the heathen districts to the north and east of the sea of Galilee; and when they did reach Galilee once more, their life was one of constant movement. Nor was it long before they again sought the shelter of a region where neither Antipas nor the Pharisees were so likely to be troublesome. Southern Palestine was practically closed to them (*St. John* vii. 1); so they turned northwards a second time to Caesarea Philippi, a town with which it has been said that in romantic beauty 'no spot in Palestine can compare.' (*St. Mark* vii. 31–viii. 27.)

One of the very greatest questions of our Lord's whole life now had to be faced and answered, though the answer had to come, not from himself, but from his followers. The apostles had long known him as a man of the most deep and sincere religion, as a master of the spiritual life, as an unapproachable pattern of sheer positive goodness, and as a personality of unearthly power and grandeur. Already they had lost faith in any other leader, and dimly appreciated that he must be the chosen Messiah (*St. John* vi. 66–9). But his conduct puzzled, and even somewhat frightened them. They could not understand why he should

The Apostles' Faith

sometimes work a stupendous miracle, as when he fed the crowds or walked upon the sea, and yet should be so sparing of his powers, so hesitant in the application of them. They could not feel assured of that still greater power which is exercised in the restraint of power. Having lost all other confidence, they had not yet found absolute faith in him.

Jesus took them to Caesarea Philippi to decide their answer. As they walked alone, after a halt when he had prayed, he turned and asked them frankly what were the speculations and superstitions current concerning him. In asking this he called himself by the title by which he alone was accustomed to name himself, 'the Son of Man'—a title which had been applied in certain Jewish writings to the expected celestial Messiah, but by no means clearly or necessarily indicated any extraordinary claims. Then he proceeded with the question at which they must have caught their breath and trembled: 'But whom say ye that I am?' And looking on that holy face, so steady, penetrating, and loving, Peter, the best and sanest common man that Christ had found in Jewry, took the plunge for all and answered boldly, 'Thou art the Christ, the Son of the living God.'

Two things Christ could now do which he had not been able to do before. He told them at once that he would be persecuted and killed, and would thereafter rise again from the dead. This necessity the apostles simply and completely failed to realize; never till Easter Day were they able to understand that their faith must reach beyond the grave. And six days later he took the most intimate three, Peter, their leader, with James, the first of the eleven to die, and John, the last of them, up amid the snows of Mount Hermon, and there revealed to them a foretaste of his glory. Never after this could their faith, however shaken, fail; and never after this could they lose the fundamental vision, however far it might fade into the background, that his kingdom was a spiritual kingdom, his glory that of another world overflowing into this. (*St. Mark* viii. 27–ix. 13; *St. Matt.* xvi. 13–xvii. 13.)

Immediately after the Transfiguration Christ returned to settle his affairs at home. How long he had known of his inevitable death we have absolutely no means of telling; probably he always knew it. But now his work was safe; he had a rock on which to build his Church; and he came back to Capernaum to bid his home farewell, secretly, lest anything should mar the tenderness of that occasion. It nearly was marred, by a childish squabble of his beloved apostles. Christ called a real child to his arms, and bade them be at peace. (*St. Mark* ix. 30–50.) Outside the apostolic circle he found derision from the brethren who were not yet spiritual brethren; but peace reigned within (*St. John* vii. 2–9). It was now autumn, and he had still six months before his passion ; but in that time he never set foot in Galilee again.

URING the six months he went to Jerusalem twice, and near it once. The first time was immediately after the events last recorded. Christ attended the feast of Tabernacles, and an ineffectual attempt was made by the Pharisees to have him arrested. However, he taught fearlessly in the Temple, taking as texts the ceremonies of the golden pitcher of water and the illuminations, which probably involved a mystical commemoration of the water struck from the rock and the pillar of fire in the book of *Exodus*, whereby the Israelites were saved in the wilderness. When he insisted on the need for genuine moral freedom, the Jews called him a Samaritan (that is, heretic), and said he was possessed—possession meaning to the Jew not merely affliction sent by God but control by the powers of evil. They also tried to stone him, but he avoided them. (*St. John* vii. 14–52, viii. 12–59.)

Afterwards, on the sabbath, he healed and converted a man born blind, to the fury of the Pharisees ; but Christ made good his point, which was that he alone could cure blindness, whether it were physical, or, as in their own case, spiritual. Nothing could convince them that any one who disagreed with their particular shibboleths was not inspired by the devil; they identified the cause of religion with the success of their own caste. Christ replied with that sublime illustration of patient humility and love for human kind, the parable of the Good Shepherd; prophesying his own death. Then he retired, probably beyond the Jordan. (*St. John* ix. 1–x. 18; compare *St. Mark* x. 1.)

Two months later, in December, he again came up to the capital for the feast of Dedication. The Jews (that is, in *St. John*, the hostile Jews) challenged him to throw off his air of detachment and say plainly whether or not he claimed to be the Messiah. The question was only a trap, and argument with them was useless, since each party approached the question of the Messiahship, and of religion in general, with absolutely opposed principles of judgement. Christ stated this very simply in the words, 'Ye believe not, because ye are not of my sheep.' For the rest, he reiterated his old appeal to them to consider whether the underlying principles on which his life and work stood, were not manifestly inspired by the good God. This they reckoned blasphemy; and Jesus, after some risk of stoning, crossed the Jordan once more, and waited. Meanwhile visitors went out there to him, and he converted many. (*St. John* x. 22–42.)

Three Visits

Weeks passed again, when another opportunity occurred for our Lord to vindicate his power of doing right and making whole. He had three dear friends living at Bethany, close to Jerusalem: Mary, Martha, and their brother Lazarus. A message was brought that Lazarus was sick. Christ waited two days, and then told the apostles that Lazarus was dead, and that he was going to Bethany to raise him from the dead. The apostles protested that it meant certain death for himself to venture near Jerusalem, but Christ set out. For all his human faith and resolution, the sorrow of death was heavily overshadowing him, and when he met the sisters mourning, sympathy for human sorrow overflowed, and Jesus wept. But faith springs deeper in the heart even than sorrow. Christ demanded a confidence which physical death could not shake, and claimed a power superior to the arbitrary barrier of the grave. 'I am the resurrection and the life: he that believeth on me, though he die, yet shall he live: and whosoever liveth and believeth on me shall never die. Believest thou this?' So for the glory of God, and that the Son of God might be glorified, he went to the tomb and called the dead man out.

The deed did not seal Christ's fate, for the Pharisees had already determined to silence him in the only effective way. But it gave them a lever with their cautious aristocratic

24 The Messianic Challenge

rivals, the Sadducean high-priestly families. They convinced them that our Lord's persistent opposition to religious authority could only end in a political revolution. The Sadducees would run no risk of that happening. The whole Sanhedrin began to take steps for Christ's destruction; and he himself went into hiding in the wild country north-east of Jerusalem. (*St. John* xi.)

ERY soon after the time arrived when pilgrims who intended to be present at the passover were moving towards Jerusalem. Jesus also moved towards the capital, not in secret, but openly. He joined the main road at Jericho, and as he passed through the town, surrounded by his Galilean adherents, he healed a blind beggar who hailed him by the Messianic title, Son of David. Then he stopped short in the road, in order to invite himself to lodge with the chief of the local tax-collectors —a profession hated by every Jewish nationalist because of its extortion and its acquiescence in the hated rule of the foreign Empire. Finally, our Lord spoke a parable which, while it certainly inculcated sober patience with regard to the expected Messianic kingdom, yet contained a possibly significant allusion to the downfall of subjects who hated their king. All this was indeed to take up the threads of

The Messianic Challenge 25

the Galilean mission which had been discarded in the previous spring, exactly a year before; and the people's old enthusiasm flared into life once again. (*St. Luke* xviii. 35–xix. 27.)

Christ spent one night at Bethany. He knew this was the end. Before setting out for the feast he had told his followers so; and now he repeated to his friends, that Mary's ointment was employed 'against the day of his burying' (*St. John* xii. 1–8). Next day he sent for a young ass, and deliberately fulfilled the Messianic expectation uttered by the prophet Zechariah, by riding upon it into the city. In these days Jesus seems to have made every effort to indicate his intention of fulfilling such details of Messianic action as a student of the Old Testament Scriptures might expect to see realized. The pilgrims broke into rejoicing; throwing their coats into the road, and strewing his path with branches from the trees, they escorted him with Messianic hymns into Jerusalem.

Promptly our Lord entered the Temple courts, and repeated the challenge with which his public career had opened. Having purged his Father's house of its money-getting parasites he taught there boldly, secure in the goodwill of the Galilean pilgrims. The Sanhedrin was powerless to intervene, for fear of provoking an outbreak. (*St. Luke* xix. 29–48.)

Yet they did what they could. Every night Jesus went out to the Mount of Olives; but

26 The Messianic Challenge

in the day-time he taught in the Temple, casting aside all reserve, and by his parables, now but a thin disguise for what was in all men's minds, challenging the position of the Pharisees and chief priests. They therefore sent spies to ask him the most awkward questions they could think of, in the hope either of embroiling him with the Roman authorities on a charge of disloyalty, or of wringing from him some admission which might be made to furnish an accusation of religious treason against Judaism, and so detach the sympathies of the pilgrims. Christ, however, triumphantly rebutted the assault. (*St. Luke* xx.)

It is abundantly clear that the character of our Lord's challenge remained unaltered. He claimed the allegiance of all his hearers to a spiritual religion of which he himself was the supreme revelation. Speaking to his disciples privately, he plainly taught two great facts. One was that the Jewish nation would be blotted out and the Temple destroyed; and this within the lifetime of the generation to which he was addressing himself. Evident signs of the catastrophe would warn those who had eyes to see. The other was that the end of this world and of normal secular life, commonly expected to take place at the Messiah's coming, was to be clearly distinguished in thought from the national catastrophe. The signs of this second event

The Messianic Challenge 27

would be no less evident, though different in kind from those preceding the fall of Jerusalem; but not even he himself could tell when it would happen. Only they must be patient and cautious in their expectation of it, and realize that their own immediate future would be one of bitter persecution. (*St. Luke* xxi.; the two events are still more clearly distinguished in *St. Mark* xiii.)

The week of preparation before the feast was passing, and still, for all the enthusiasm with which the nationalist multitudes had welcomed his renewed activity, Jesus failed to put himself at their head to prosecute a forward movement. He did no public miracle: he only talked his old amazing but inconclusive talk. One of the twelve, Judas Iscariot, lost patience. He had no mind to be persecuted; he had only joined the movement for the hope of what he could make out of it for himself. Judas decided (rightly) that in a material sense he stood to gain nothing by further discipleship. So he went to the Sanhedrin and sold his Master, promising to let them know Christ's movements, so that when a chance occurred they might arrest him quietly. Jesus knew it; but the objects which he sought were not material. His challenge to the Jews was the challenge of spiritual reality against materialism; Judas's action, though he was a 'devil,' only brought matters to a sharper and more decisive crisis or judgement. So Christ

28 The Messianic Challenge

ignored the treachery. (*St. John* vi. 70, xii. 4–6, 31–3 ; *St. Luke* xxii. 3–6.)

On the Thursday (the passover began on the Friday evening), in response to a request from his disciples (*St. Mark* xiv. 12), our Lord sent two of them to make preparation for the passover which he knew himself he would not eat (*St. Luke* xxii. 15, 16). The Synoptic gospels give the impression that he actually did eat the passover, but it is clear from *St. John* that he suffered on the afternoon before the festival. The last supper on the Thursday took the place for that little band of the Jewish sacrificial feast. And well it might ; for at that supper Jesus instituted the Christian sacrifice of the holy Mass and fed his followers for the first time with the bread of life ; presenting before God in a prophetic manner the sacrifice of his sacred body, which was destined to be made on the morrow, and pleading the adorable offering of his blood even before it had actually been shed upon the cross. (*St. Luke* xxii. 14–23.)

After supper Judas was dismissed, and Jesus gave his last farewell to the apostles. Again and again he told them to support their faith by the exercise of that practical love which is displayed in obedience ; and promised them that if they were obedient the Spirit of his own life, the Holy Spirit, should direct and possess their lives also, and make his own presence with them felt. Then they

Passion and Resurrection 29

all departed from the upper room where the supper had been eaten, and crossed the city in the darkness. Jesus prayed both for his followers and for their future converts. (*St. John* xiii.–xvii.)

Arrived at a favourite resting place, the garden of Gethsemane, Jesus prayed in a human agony that he might be spared the awful test of moral endurance which was to follow. Then he rose, stedfast and secure, to fulfil the will of God. Lights and the jangle of weapons broke the peace of the garden. It was Judas, with the officers of the Sanhedrin and a detachment of the Roman garrison which had been borrowed to make all sure. Peter charged them with single-hearted heroism; but Jesus refused to be rescued, and at that the apostles broke and fled. The stage was now set for the judgement. (*St. John* xviii. 1–12; *St. Luke* xxii. 39–53.)

UR Lord was haled first before the ex-high priest Annas, and there examined as to his claims. He refused to give the evidence they sought against himself, until the high priest solemnly and formally asked him, 'Art thou the Christ (that is, Messiah)?' Our Lord at once replied that he was, and added that hereafter he would sit at God's right hand and be seen coming in the clouds of heaven—a clear claim to be the Judge at

whose coming the present positions of prisoner and of accusers would be reversed. That was enough. After savage ill-treatment he was sent at dawn before a formal meeting of the Sanhedrin at the house of Caiaphas, the high priest recognized by the Roman government. Thence he was hurried before the Roman governor, who alone had the power of life and death. (*St. John* xviii. 12–32 ; *St. Mark* xiv. 53–xv. 1.)

Over twenty years before, Judaea and all southern Palestine had been taken from the Herods and put under a Roman official. The present governor was Pontius Pilatus, corrupt, reckless, superstitious, cowardly. The majesty of Christ, and his obvious moral and spiritual superiority to his accusers, aroused Pilate's dread, and he tried every means of shifting the responsibility for condemning him, or of placating the Jews with something short of the death penalty. But Herod (Antipas) failed his hopes, and the Jewish leaders would neither be content with his scourging Christ nor accept our Lord's release as a concession to the religious occasion.

The accusation made was a vague one, that Christ's teaching caused social disturbance, and had political objects. When pressed, the Jews had to admit that his real offence was against religion, not the State. But they threatened to report to Rome that Pilate failed to condemn one who claimed a revolutionary Jewish kingship, which was flat treason; and the governor's resistance collapsed. Christ was taken to Mount Calvary, and crucified between two murderers. There was no riot. The pilgrims, like Judas, saw their hopes had been illusions, not because Christ was attacked, but because he did not retaliate. 'He saved others; himself he cannot save. Let the Christ now come down from the cross, that we may see and believe.' (*St. Luke* xxiii.; *St. John* xviii. 33–xix. 42.)

The hill of Calvary was the true court of judgement; the cross of Christ reveals the judgement which men's own lives and the state of their souls automatically carry with them. The spiritual and the worldly, obedience and selfishness, are there distinguished by an effective touchstone. Not for nothing was Christ lifted between earth and heaven, and set between a ruffian and a penitent. 'Ye judge after the flesh; I judge no man.' Yet 'for judgement came I into this world' (*St. John* viii. 15, ix. 39).

The scandalous unrighteousness of the proceedings brought into the open two members of the Sanhedrin who were secret disciples, Nicodemus, and Joseph of Arimathaea. They buried Christ with all the reverence that time allowed. But on the morning of the Sunday, when the faithful women went to make further provision, they found the tomb open and empty; two apostles investigating found the

Passion and Resurrection

grave-clothes discarded. Visions were seen by some of persons taken to be angels, who asserted that the Lord of life had risen from the dead. And then began a series of occasions upon which Jesus himself appeared, now to one or two, now to the eleven, in Jerusalem; but always to believers only. Then, on the return of the disciples to Galilee, he renewed their vocation by a repetition of the miracle which had marked the first call of four of them to become fishers of men. Here, too, probably, it was that he appeared to above five hundred disciples at once (1 *Cor.* xv. 6).

Finally, after forty days of evidence by which he fully convinced all those who had known him best that he himself, body and soul, had truly risen from the grave, having sent the apostles back to Jerusalem, their future headquarters, and given them such directions as they needed, he led them out to the Mount of Olives. There, in the act of blessing them, he was taken up into the air and a cloud enveloped him, veiling the passage of his flesh from earthly humiliation to spiritual glory. In the figurative language which can alone be used of unexperienced heavenly events, the Son of God sat down at God's right hand, there to reign over his Church in heaven, at rest, and in the world, from everlasting God, and now to everlasting Man. (*St. Luke* xxiv.; *St. John* xx.–xxi.; *St. Matt.* xxviii.; *Acts* i. 1–14.)

*A Short History of
The Catholic Church*

THE CONGRESS BOOKS : No. 11

A SHORT HISTORY OF THE CATHOLIC CHURCH

W. H. HUTTON, D.D.
Dean of Winchester

LONDON
THE SOCIETY OF
SS. PETER & PAUL
32 *George St., Hanover Sq., W.* 1, *and
The Abbey House, Westminster, S.W.* 1

A Short History of the Catholic Church

OUR Lord Jesus Christ, the only-begotten Son of God, who for us men and for our salvation came down from heaven, and was incarnate by the Holy Ghost of the Virgin Mary, and was made man, founded on earth a holy Church to carry on his work among men. This was not merely the ancient Church, in which the Jews had received the revelation of God, adapted to the needs of a new age: it came down out of heaven as a bride adorned for her husband, a new creation inspired for all time by the Holy Spirit; and it was, as St. Paul declared, the very body of the Lord Christ living and working among human beings.

Our Lord during his earthly life was surrounded by a body of disciples and an inner circle of intimate friends, his twelve apostles, to whom he revealed his teaching and with whom, after his resurrection, he spent forty days, speaking of the things pertaining to the kingdom of God. After his ascension the apostles, with the blessed Virgin, awaited a

6   Spread of the Church

promised out-pouring of the Holy Spirit. When he descended upon them, on the day of Pentecost (known in later days in English as the first Whit Sunday) the Church started on her work as the pillar and ground of the truth revealed from age to age.

Thus the history of the Catholic Church begins with the day of Pentecost, probably May 28, A.D. 29, when the ' kingdom of heaven' was founded among men. From the first it was ruled by the apostles of our Lord, among whom one, chosen by lot under the guidance of the Spirit, replaced the traitor Judas. They were to be witnesses of the Resurrection, the great act of divine power which showed that the Lord was living, and that he had brought life and immortality to light through the gospel. From that moment began the missionary work which should in God's good time bring the world to the feet of Christ.

To St. Peter, the chief of the apostles, first came the revelation that all nations were to be admitted to the Christian fellowship. And the new convert, Saul of Tarsus, became, as Paul the Christian, the leader of the great adventure. The dispersion of the first disciples brought the gospel to the Jews scattered throughout the Roman world. Thus we may trace in the Acts of the Apostles and in the epistles of St. Paul (some of which are the earliest Christian writings we now possess) how the mission spread throughout all lands accessible from the central home of the disciples of the Lord. At first this centre was Jerusalem. Then a new centre arose at Antioch, where the name of Christians was first borne by the followers of our Lord. And so the teaching spread, and the Church grew in order and stability.

It grew through its organization, and through its martyrs. The Church's ministry consisted of (*a*) temporary and general, and (*b*) permanent and local, officials. The first consisted of the apostles, who were witnesses of the Lord's resurrection and had derived their powers directly from himself, and of other ' prophets,' men endowed with special gifts of revelation and exposition, who belonged to the first age of the Church. The second included the three Orders of bishops, priests¹ and deacons, which endure to this day. This threefold ministry was partly developed out of an earlier one, in which the bishops (' overseers,' *episcopoi*) seem to have been reckoned as identical with the priests (' elders,' *presbuteroi*). The deacons were from the apostles' time an inferior order of the ministry, concerned with work less distinctively spiritual. But within a very short time, from early in the second century, all three orders were distinct. The bishops had jurisdiction, generally local; the priests had authority to minister the sacraments; the deacons were assistants.

8 Its Bible

Later on 'minor' orders appeared, not indelible, and conferred on persons not permanently devoted to definite religious work: these the Church has used or disused, from time to time, in different ages and different parts of the world. There were also deaconesses, women set apart for the special instruction and edification of their own sex and of children, but with duties also in the Church at large. They may be grouped for convenience with the 'minor' orders of ministers, as they were never reckoned as 'sacred ministers' in the same sense as are the members of the three 'major' orders of men.

Such was the Church to which was entrusted 'the oracles of God': and so she started on her way, with her organization and her literature, the latter consisting of the Scriptures of the Old Testament and such writings of the first Christian age as were recognized as containing the further revelation of God for the guidance of the world.

Her path was from the first in some degree a way of sorrows. The Jews stoned Stephen, who called upon Jesus as his Saviour and God, and Herod Agrippa had James beheaded. When the new religion spread through the Roman Empire, after a short period of surprised and contemptuous tolerance it was regarded as a political danger, and adherence to it was punished with death. Occasional persecutions arose early: but from A.D. 98

Martyrs & Apologists

for about a century persecution was, if not always violent, at any rate automatic and continuous, and there were many martyrs who gave up their lives rather than deny the Godhead of Jesus Christ, from St. Peter and St. Paul, martyred at Rome before the end of the first century, to St. Ignatius and St. Polycarp, and many others as noble but less famous. Attacked thus from without, the Church had also to withstand false teaching within. There were many varieties of 'Gnostics,' whose teaching was a many-sided and fantastic perversion of the faith once for all delivered to the Church, not unlike modern theosophy. And there were ascetic sects, Marcionites, Montanists, and others, whose extreme views somewhat resembled certain of the Anabaptist doctrines in the sixteenth century. These two-fold attacks were met by the first Christian 'Apologists,' defenders of the faith on moral, historical, and philosophic grounds.

Thus not only was the blood of martyrs the seed of the Church, but the persistent preaching and writing of her disciples caught more and more the ear of the outside world. The centre of thought shifted westwards. From Rome radiated the political influence which ruled the world. There St. Peter and St. Paul had been martyred. Thence at the seat of imperial government came the wisest and ablest leaders of the Church. The bishops

10 Conversion of Constantine

of Rome, successors of St. Peter and of that St. Clement who wrote a letter, still existing, to the Corinthians, found their advice sought by all parts of Christendom. Rome began to be as important in Church as in State. In time, to be in communion with Rome became as important as to be in subjection to the Empire.

THE reigns of the Emperors Decius (249–51), Valerian (253–60), and Diocletian (284–305) were marked by new and most fierce persecutions of the whole Church. To this last period probably belongs the first British martyr, St. Alban. It was followed by a great extension of the Church. The Emperor Constantine in 313 found it impossible to withstand her growing influence. Probably already himself persuaded to be a Christian, he issued in that year the Edict of Milan, which placed Christianity in a position of equality with the imperial religion. Christianity had already spread over a very large part of Asia and extended through North Africa and Italy to Gaul, Spain, and Britain. The leading influence was still undoubtedly Eastern, and the chief theologians were Greek: but the Church was as certainly Catholic, that is Universal, in her appeal and her expansion.

The time of the great Church Councils now

The Great Councils

began with the Synod of Arles, held to meet the dangerous contentions of the Donatists, a fanatical sect which seemed likely to control the Christianity of Africa. More dangerous still was the teaching of Arius, who denied the eternal Godhead of the Son. Constantine the Emperor summoned a Council of the whole Church at Nicaea, in 325. About 300 bishops were present, and a creed was drawn up which declared the Son to be of one substance (*homo-ousios*) with the Father. When Constantine died in 337 it may be said that the whole Roman world was nominally Christian, and that the Christianity it professed was Catholic, that is, it accepted the teaching of the Church which was inherited from the apostles.

But the victory was not yet won. In the middle of the fourth century Arianism gained an enormous, though temporary, increase of strength, being supported by many worldly bishops and half-converted politicians; and later on the Emperor Julian became an apostate, and persecuted the Church, though that was not for long. But still the theologians, even when they were persecuted (and even more when they were not), contended over the Church's doctrine, which needed, as time went on, to be made clear in its relation to the thought and the needs of the secular world. Thus came an age when more Church Councils had to define the faith. So (among many

The Great Fathers

others) we have, after the great Council of Nicaea in 325, three others which declared our Lord's 'deity, his manhood, the conjunction of both, and the distinction of the one from the other' (Hooker, *Ecclesiastical Polity*, V. liv. 10). These were the second General Council at Constantinople in 381, the third General Council at Ephesus in 431, and the fourth General Council at Chalcedon in 451. The decisions of the first had declared, against Arius, that our Lord is *truly* God : the second, against Apollinaris, stated that he is *perfectly* Man : the third, against Nestorius, that he is *indivisibly* God and Man : and the fourth, against Eutyches, that he is *distinctly* both.

The age of the Councils was also the age of the great Fathers, by whose writings the faith of the Church was confirmed. Among other important theologians were St. Athanasius, the great exponent of the doctrine of the Incarnation ; St. Basil, the great writer on the Holy Spirit ; St. Cyril, a great theological teacher ; St. Jerome, great as a controversialist, and the most famous translator of the Scriptures into Latin ; St. Chrysostom, the greatest preacher of the church of Constantinople ; St. Clement, St. Leo, St. Gregory the Great, in different centuries bishops of Rome and vindicators of the Church's faith ; St. Ambrose at Milan, and St. Augustine in North Africa, profoundly influencing the

Rise of the Papacy

theology of later ages. And as the Church grew in extent and in power a new organization sprang up in monasticism ; assemblies of men, and also of women, were founded to engage in perpetual worship, living a common life, unmarried, secluded from the world. St. Basil in the East, and St. Benedict in the West, gave monastic Rules which have been followed ever since their day.

The higher government of the Church now came to be fixed under four patriarchates : in the East, Jerusalem, Antioch, and Constantinople ; the last now the seat of the Emperor of the Roman World, its patriarch claiming a practical equality with Rome, the ruling see in the West. From the sixth century, while the claims of Constantinople were never abated, the power of Rome grew. When there was no longer a Roman Emperor in the city, the pope of Rome succeeded to not a little of his powers. Political authority, never claimed by the see of Constantinople, came more and more to the front among the Roman prelates : and when after a long abeyance the Empire of the West was revived under a Frankish Caesar, Charles the Great, in 800, a large part of the imperial power was seen to have slipped into the hands of the Western patriarch. From 500 to 1500 it may be said that the popes were claiming authority over the Christian world ; and the claim met with a large measure of success.

14   Christian Missions

But no less, while the monks gave new life and new learning to the Church, radiating their influence from St. Benedict's monastery of Monte Cassino, the papacy not long after Gregory the Great (590–604) fell into discredit and decay, in the hands of bad or feeble men, ruled by politicians for their own ends. A revival came about through the Emperor Charles the Great (800–14) ; and again, with even greater necessity, through Otto I (962–73) and his successors, German princes who held the imperial crown of Rome, and a great pope, Sylvester II (999–1003).

Christianity had now spread practically over all Europe. Gaul was a great Christian country with kings in alliance with the Church. Britain, where Christianity had first come under the Romans, but had been practically blotted out by the invasion of heathen Saxons, was now converted through a mission from Rome (under St. Augustine of Canterbury) and a mission from Iona (the monastery of St. Columba)—for Ireland and Scotland already knew of the faith of Christ. In the East, Christian missions (sometimes heretical, especially those belonging to the Monophysites—people who taught that our Lord's divine and human natures became one—and Nestorians and Arians) spread very far, and much that is now desert was Christian. Already there were many Christians, particularly in the Far East, who did not belong to the Catholic Church. With them this short history has no concern, and later on they lost most of their importance. In the seventh century many Christian possessions were conquered by the Persians, but their victories were ended when the Emperor Heraclius in 629 won back the Holy Cross, believed to have been discovered three centuries before by Helena, the mother of Constantine, to the church of the Resurrection at Jerusalem.

A more serious danger was the appearance in Arabia of a new religion (which owed something to the Jews and the Nestorians) founded by Muhammad in 622. By the middle of the seventh century his followers had attacked the Church and Empire in North Africa, and within fifty years both were destroyed. Only in Abyssinia did the Church survive, ignorant and eventually heretical—and in Egypt, in the church of the Copts. A dark age befell the Church when Muhammadans and heretics swept over many of the lands where the Catholic faith had been taught; and the Roman bishops were unable and often unworthy to vindicate her. Only in the East, though the Emperors were sometimes heretical, did the Church of Constantinople hold firmly to the faith, and, conquering the practical heresy of Iconoclasm (which by attacking the reverence paid to images and pictures threatened belief in the true humanity of

Christ), remained immovable in the ancient faith, confirmed by the later Councils of the Church, and by the teaching of her great theologians, such as St. John of Damascus.

WE now begin the Middle Age, which may be said to extend from 1000 to 1500. It was marked by the growth of the papal power, by the work of a great religious philosophy, by the creation of new Religious Orders, and by a division between the East and the West which remains to this day. With regard to the last, there are two critical dates. The first was 867, when Photius, patriarch of Constantinople, repudiated the popes' claim to sovereign jurisdiction, and declared the addition to the Nicene Creed of the procession of the Holy Ghost 'from the Son' to be heretical. This schism was healed in 880, chiefly by submission on the part of Rome. For the succeeding centuries it may be said that the relation between Rome and Constantinople was one of armed neutrality. In 1054 Michael Caerularius, patriarch of Constantinople, and Leo IX, pope of Rome, came to a final disagreement, in which minor matters of doctrine were mixed up with the Roman claim for universal submission ; and the East determined to preserve

Papal Claims

its ancient freedom. For the lands between Germany and Thrace both Eastern and Western missionaries contended, and churches were founded which looked to Rome or Constantinople for rule.

In 1439, when the Muhammadan Turks had made almost all the Eastern Empire their prey, a Council at Florence, attended by the Emperor and the patriarch, accepted the papal claims, saving the rights and privileges of the patriarchs of the East ; and for a brief space the Catholic Church was reunited. When in 1453 Constantinople fell to the Turks, the Greeks returned to their ecclesiastical independence, and they have remained, in the five hundred years that have followed, stedfast in the faith of the General Councils without addition or loss.

Throughout all these years and the whole of the Middle Age, the power of the popes grew, through great popes like Gregory VII (1073–85) who made claim to rule all the ecclesiastical relations of the civil power as the vicegerent of Christ, Innocent III (1198–1216) who extended this claim far into the realm of politics, and Boniface VIII (1294–1303) who attempted to win an entire independence for the clergy, and advanced the papal assertions to a point where it was certain they would be resisted by all the secular powers. The claims were based upon Decretals, forged in the interests of Rome by some ecclesiastical

18 Papal Schisms

lawyers, and accepted by the Church for centuries as authentic.

But in the Middle Age the popes never succeeded in establishing an uncontrolled power, chiefly through the fact of the Great Schism of the fourteenth century, when rival claimants to the papacy contended for the allegiance of the faithful, and owing to the occasional assertions of authority by General Councils in the Church. Clement V (1305–14) left Rome and moved the seat of government to Avignon, where the popes were in exile under the influence of France till 1378. Hardly was this over before the Great Schism began, when rival popes claimed to have been lawfully elected to the see of St. Peter (1378): even now the Church has not decided which was the true pope, Urban VI or Clement VII. While popes contended, cardinals endeavoured to save the Church, and summoned a Council at Pisa in 1409, which deposed two popes and elected another. The successor of this third, John XXIII, with the Emperor Sigismund, summoned the Council of Constance, 1414–18, which condemned the Bohemian reformer Hus and crushed the movement for reform which had shown itself in many parts of the Church, but ended the Great Schism by the election of pope Martin V (1417). The only results of this period of Councils were the failure of the Church, as represented by her bishops in council, to control the

Scholastic Philosophy 19

papacy, the corruption of the Western Church at its Roman centre, and the inevitable coming of a Reformation which should take the form of a still greater schism than had ever been known before.

At Rome the re-establishment of the papal power coincided with a Renaissance of the ancient learning which the Middle Age had forgotten—too often also of the low ancient standards of morals. The papacy itself became almost as corrupt as it had been in the tenth century. Then came the Reformation, which transformed the religious aspect of Europe. But the Middle Age left two important legacies, a religious philosophy and the Religious Orders.

Of the first it may briefly be said that the age of the Schoolmen was a period of definitely Christian philosophy. Founding themselves upon what they could learn of the ancient philosophers, Christian scholars thought out the metaphysical bases of the Catholic faith, and met the questionings of their day with a reasoned presentation of the Church's truth. Such were Alexander Hales (*d*. 1245); Albertus Magnus (*d*. 1208); St. Thomas Aquinas (*d*. 1274), whose *Summa Theologiae* is still the greatest exposition of Catholic philosophy; St. Bonaventura (*d*. 1274); and Roger Bacon (*d*. 1294); and earlier than any of these the great St. Anselm, archbishop of Canterbury (*d*. 1109), whose treatise on the Incarnation

The Religious Orders

(*Cur Deus Homo*) was for long the most famous exposition of the doctrine.

These men belonged to the great Religious Orders, whose foundation and growth belong to the Middle Age. The rule of St. Benedict, the real founder of Western monasticism, in the sixth century, received a new vitality through the devotion of the abbey of Cluny in Burgundy in the eleventh century; and thence there spread over Europe a number of congregations which strictly observed the constitutions of the founder. In times of war and licence new orders sprang into existence to meet the evils of the age. Such were the Carthusians, the Cistercians (of whom the most famous member was St. Bernard of Clairvaux), both of these containing not only men in holy orders but a large number of lay brethren; and the two great military orders of the Hospital and the Temple, founded for the succour and defence of the Holy Land; and others fighting against infidels in Germany and Spain.

The Church indeed in the Middle Age, through its lay members, was often literally militant. Not only were the Muhammadans gradually driven out of Spain, of which they had conquered nearly the whole on the decay of the Roman Empire, but they were attacked in their eastern strongholds in many attempts to win back for the Church of Christ the land where he shed his blood, and the countries

The Crusades

which had first accepted the teachings of his apostles.

These great adventures, inspired by great preachers and led by great kings, are known as the Crusades. The first conquered Nicaea and Antioch, and on July 15, 1099, captured Jerusalem, where it set up a Christian kingdom: the second, preached by St. Bernard, endeavoured with little success to win back what had been lost in the half century after the first conquest: the third, in which the Emperor Frederick I (who was drowned), Philip Augustus, king of the Franks, and Richard Cœur de Lion, king of the English, took part, tried to win back Jerusalem, which had been taken by Saladin in A.D. 1187, but only succeeded in retaining the coast of Palestine for the Christians, with free access to the Holy City. The fourth turned aside, with incredible baseness, to conquer Constantinople and set up there a Latin Empire. In the fifth, St. Louis IX of France made two gallant attempts to shake the Muhammadan power, but with little success; and a little later Edward, afterwards king of England, made the same venture. The Crusades, at least for a time, stemmed the infidel advance, and ultimately prevented its extension in Europe; they also did much to unite the West under the popes, who alone could join together the discordant elements of which their armies were composed.

The Friars

But the Church was not only militant with human weapons. She fought with the sword of the Spirit : not only through the monks and the philosophers, but also through the new Orders called friars, which came into existence in the twelfth century under the leadership of two great saints, St. Francis of Assisi and St. Dominic. These noble men set themselves to minister to the outcasts and to help the parish priests in preaching and by teaching. The Franciscans and the Dominicans put new life into the Church, and beside them grew up Orders of women, which produced such noble lives as those of St. Clare, St. Catherine of Siena, and St. Catherine of Genoa.

By such support, and in such circumstances, the papacy reached the power which it held at the end of the Middle Age. Rome was the centre of Christian life, and it had become the resort of all who sought the solution of theological, or legal, or practical questions affecting the life of the Church. There were great and good popes, as well as some wicked ones and others the dependants of emperors and kings. But the Church which they maintained survived the days of subjection, of exile, and of contempt, and stood forth, in spite of grave corruptions, at the head of Western Christendom when a new and very different age dawned upon the world.

The Protestant Revolt 23

BY the end of the fifteenth century the Church was felt on all sides to need a real reform. Unhappily when this came it involved a revolution. Till the year 1517 heresies and revolts, even if strong for a time, like that of Bohemia, were repressed with no great difficulty. The Church, but for the claims of the pope which caused the schism between East and West, was at one in all fundamental doctrines. The sacraments and the ministry stood on foundations accepted by the whole Church.

But now came a far more disastrous schism. From 1517, when a friar named Martin Luther nailed up on the church of Wittenberg an attack upon some of the practical teaching of the Roman Church, there was a division which split off from the ancient Church a great part of Christendom. This is that cataclysm which rent Europe in twain and is known as the Reformation. It created two great groups of anti-Catholic teaching, founded by Luther in Germany and by Zwinglius and Calvin in Switzerland, whose followers, abandoning the teaching of the Church on the sacraments and the ministry, obtained religious control in great parts of Germany, France, and Scandinavia, largely influenced England, and almost entirely subjugated Scotland. In Sweden, though much of the doctrine of these Protestants (a name given through a famous declaration of revolt at Augsburg) was accepted, an attempt was made to preserve the episcopal succession which had always been regarded as essential in the Catholic Church.

In England the transmission of holy orders and the succession of episcopal sees was unbroken, through periods first of rejection, then of re-acceptance, and then of final rejection, of the papal claims. When the pope excommunicated Queen Elizabeth and declared that her subjects were freed from allegiance to her, the rift between England and Rome became complete, and the breach has never been repaired. The English Church became isolated from the main current of Western Catholicity; but it never abandoned Catholic faith and orders, and it asserted its determination not ' to separate from the unity of Christ's Catholic Church.' The Eastern Church held on its orthodox way, untouched by the torrent of Western change; the English, while repudiating the claims of Rome, refrained from any reflection upon the Great Church of Constantinople; and, as the centuries have gone on, after various attempts at closer association, the Church of England has in the twentieth century had the validity of its ministry, as that of part of the Catholic Church, freely recognized by that ancient and unchanging patriarchate.

But the Reformation which profoundly

Roman Catholic Revival 25

affected the Church in the sixteenth century was by no means only Protestant or Anglican. The Churches which remained in communion with Rome did much, each of them, to set its house in order. In Spain, Italy, France, and Southern Germany new life came to the Church through the work of new Religious Orders, eminent theologians, and devoted saints. Most famous of the creations of the Reforming era in the Roman Church was the Society of Jesus, founded by St. Ignatius of Loyola (1491–1566) to be, in his own words, 'like a cohort gathered to fight spiritual enemies as men devoted body and soul to our Lord Jesus Christ, and his vicar on earth,' the pope. The Jesuits as teachers and as missionaries gave new power to the Roman Church. There has been no greater missionary than St. Francis Xavier (1506–52) whose body rests at Goa in Portuguese India. But their intervention in politics made them unpopular among the Catholic secular powers, and they were dissolved by the pope as dangerous to the Church in 1773; but the Society was revived, before many years had passed, when Europe was changed by the French Revolution.

The Reformation era was marked also by a great Council at Trent, which represented only the bodies in communion with Rome (1545–64). This stereotyped the doctrine of the Church of Rome of that time, as necessary to salvation, following the declaration of Boniface VIII in 1302 that 'it is altogether necessary to salvation for every human creature to be subject to the Roman pontiff.' Thus the position of the papacy was asserted in opposition to England and to the Orthodox East.

From the beginning of the seventeenth century it may be said that political interests less and less affected the growth of the Church in Europe, and thus she was able to pursue her way, under the guidance of different leaders.

While we do not doubt our Lord's promise to be with his Church till the end of the world, and know that his Spirit is ever guiding her into all the truth, we must, in the divided condition of his Visible Body, look for the complete expression of his will only to that teaching which is held by the whole Church, Eastern and Western. The Catholic doctrine of the sacraments is that on which the whole Church is agreed. The Catholic ministry is that which fulfils the conditions which from the first age have been declared to be essential. But anything which is taught exclusively by the Roman Church, or the Eastern Churches, or the Churches in communion with the Church of England, is not part of that Catholic faith to which a man must hold who wishes to be in a state of salvation.

This must be borne in mind when we study

Church and State 27

the Church history of the last three centuries. These have been chiefly marked by the extension of Christ's kingdom upon earth. Wars there have been, such as the Thirty Years' War in Germany, and the French Wars of Religion, in which different religious bodies were arrayed against each other; but they were wars of policy, not wars for or against the Catholic Church. Restrictions on Christian liberty have been fixed or removed in different countries, and there have been periods in which the Church has lost privileges which she had held under the State for centuries. But these things have not, like the changes under Constantine or Gregory the Great or Gregory VII or Henry VIII, affected the main current of the Church's progress. She has gone on her way less and less trammelled by the politics of the age.

When the French Revolution (1789–1815) swept over Europe it, for a time, dispossessed the Church in different States, and the philosophy of the period struck violent blows against religion, from which, especially in Roman Catholic countries, the faith of men and women suffered severely. But all the while, all over the Christian world, saintly lives were bearing witness to the inspiration of the Holy Spirit and the security of the Church. And missions to preach the faith of Christ to every creature have spread from every branch of the Church over the whole

28   Missionary Activity

world. The Orthodox East has wonderful missions in Asia: the Roman Church has left no country without representation of its teaching: and the English Church and the Churches in communion with her have spread far beyond the limits of the British Empire, which is geographically the greatest Empire the world has ever known. In Africa a hard battle is being fought with Muhammadanism, and Islam still holds on to a fringe of Europe, everywhere persecuting and murdering as its religion binds it to do. The noblest example of Christian faith and practice to-day is undoubtedly to be found in the Eastern Churches, where thousands have been martyred for their adherence to Christ.

The victory is very far from being won: it is delayed by the weakness and the arrogance, the contentions and the compromises, which are to be found in every branch of the Church. Against these disasters must be set the bright examples of missions which witness for Christ all over the world. When the Church, in any branch, is disheartened, let her think of the progress in the conversion of the heathen which has been made in the last hundred years, and remember that it is worthy to be placed beside the victories of the apostolic age.

There have been in these last centuries many barriers to Christian progress. Most of these may be traced to the desire of each

The Hope of Reunion 29

branch of the Church to pursue its own way in isolation. Between Rome and Canterbury there has been much bitterness and suspicion, now at length happily decreased, if not entirely done away. The Eastern Churches have too often held haughtily aloof from those of the West. But they would say that this is necessary until the removal of the barrier caused by the papal claims, which they have always from the very first rejected as not part of the Catholic faith. Their difficulty was increased by decisions of the Church of Rome in the nineteenth century, and especially by that of the Vatican Council, in 1871, that 'the definitions of the Roman pontiff are irreformable of themselves and not by the consent of the Church.' The supremacy claimed for the pope over the Councils of the whole Catholic Church is a standing and obvious barrier to reunion.

This briefly represents a summary of the Church history of the last three centuries, in which there are no great outstanding events, and few, if any, great outstanding characters. Wide though the divergence is between them, it cannot be doubted that Easterns and Romans and Anglicans are nearer to each other than they were three centuries ago; and while they hold firmly to the points which they have all maintained, points of the faith once for all delivered to the saints, they are nearer together than they recognize, and will

Conclusion

be surely led into the unity for which the Lord prayed; in which, in his time, all Christians must come to share.

Nor must we omit to praise God for his goodness in the grace given to many who do not accept the ancient faith and ministry of the Church, yet often give a noble example of Christian work and Christian character. The Catholic Church, whose history and principles descend from the earliest days, loves them, and never ceases to pray that all may come to the unity of the Spirit in the knowledge of the truth.

May God speedily renew the good estate of the Catholic Church; that all who profess and call themselves Christians may be led into the way of truth, and hold the faith in unity of spirit, in the bond of peace, and in righteousness of life.

THE CONGRESS BOOKS: No. 12

CHRIST AND CATHOLICISM

CLEMENT HOSKYNS
Fellow of Corpus Christi College, Cambridge
Examining Chaplain to the Bishop of Manchester

LONDON
THE SOCIETY OF
SS. PETER & PAUL
32 *George St., Hanover Sq., W.* 1, *and*
The Abbey House, Westminster, S.W. 1

Christ and Catholicism

AT the present time it is widely assumed that the Christianity of the New Testament and the Catholic faith are two different systems, and that the religion taught by our Lord bears no vital relation to the Catholic religion, which claims his authority. It is said that he taught a simple religion of the love of God and the love of man, that he made no peculiar claims for his own person, that he was a Jew anxious for the purification of the religion of his people, that he was crucified because he refused to compromise with the Jewish authorities, and that he lived and died as merely one, though that one the greatest, of the prophets. After his death his disciples, and St. Paul in particular, are said gradually to have deified him, invented the Church with its doctrines and sacraments and its emphasis on the miraculous, and elaborated (and, in so doing, corrupted) the simplicity of his teaching. The outcome of this development was the Catholic religion, which dominated Western civilisation till the Reformation, when Luther rediscovered something of the original religion,

Did Christ Teach Catholicism? 3

it being left for the scholars of the nineteenth century to complete his discovery. Now at last, it is claimed, the true Jesus of history has been found, and we are free of dogmas, free of the miraculous 'supernatural' additions to genuine Christianity, free of sacramental and sacrificial worship, free of the Church.

The object of this book is to point out that the characteristic notes of Catholic Christianity can be traced back to the teaching of our Lord himself, and that, therefore, his gospel was not so 'simple' as is often supposed.

Since it is generally acknowledged that St. John's gospel was written at the end of the first century, and that its choice of subject-matter and method of treatment were designed, at least in part, to illustrate Christian beliefs and practices of that time; and since it is also generally acknowledged that St. Mark's gospel was written considerably earlier, and that it preserves the most primitive tradition of our Lord's life and teaching: a comparison of these two gospels ought to reveal the main lines of development within primitive Christianity, and to enable us to judge how far this development was due to a legitimate or illegitimate interpretation of the gospel of Jesus. We will, therefore, outline the evidence of St. John's gospel as to the nature of the Christian religion at the close of the first century, and then pass on to compare this with the evidence

4 St. John a Catholic Christian

of St. Mark's gospel as to the nature of the teaching which we have every reason to believe was the teaching of our Lord himself.

THE true worship of God forms the subject of the discourse with the woman of Samaria. (*St. John* iv. 19-26.) The old centres of worship have been superseded. The hour has come, and the true and spiritual worship of God has been revealed; true and spiritual, because it is based on the knowledge of God revealed by the Messiah himself: and the Father is even now seeking the true worshippers. 'We worship what we know:' and this means, for the author and his readers, 'we Christians.' Christian worship, though it has its origin in Jewish worship, is limited to no single temple, for wherever a community of Christians exists, there is the true worship of God.

That Christian worship has superseded the old Jewish worship is implied in the narrative of the 'cleansing of the Temple.' (*St. John* ii. 13-22.) It is presumed that the reader sees in our Lord's action in the Temple a Messianic act abolishing animal sacrifice. The Jews ask him, 'What sign shewest thou unto us, seeing that thou doest these things?' In other words, what sign can he give that he is the Messiah. And St. John interprets the mysterious answer,

St. John a Catholic Christian 5

'Destroy this temple, and in three days I will raise it up,' as referring to his body, which will supersede the old animal sacrifices, and is to become the centre of the true and spiritual worship of God. This is worked out in greater detail in the discourse which follows the account of the feeding of the five thousand and leads up to the statement, 'He that eateth my flesh and drinketh my blood abideth in me, and I in him' (*St. John* vi. 56).

Actually, it is not so much the cleansing of the Temple which St. John is describing as its abolition. To him, as to the other New Testament writers, the Temple was destroyed, not by the Roman armies, but by the coming of Christianity. The Roman armies did but express materially what had been spiritually effected by the life and death of Jesus the Christ.

The Christians, who shared in this true worship, were not isolated and unorganized individuals, known only to God. They formed a visible fellowship into which men could enter, and from which they could be excluded (*St. John* iii. 5 ; compare 1 *John* ii. 18, 19 ; iv. 1.) To enter into this community was to pass from death into life, and to leave it was to pass from life into death. The parables of the Good Shepherd and of the Door of the sheep are without meaning unless this be assumed. Within the fold of the Jewish religion the sheep were cramped and confined, until Jesus,

6 St. John a Catholic Christian

the Good Shepherd, came and called the sheep, who were his, out of the old fold into a new pasturage. The image then suddenly changes, and the sheep are pictured in their new fold enjoying their new pasturage and passing freely in and out through the Door of the sheep, which is the Lord himself. (*St. John* x. 1–10.)

Conversion to Christianity thus involved not only partaking in the new worship of God, but also incorporation into the one new community or fellowship or Church. No limit of race or religion was imposed, for the Christian Church was open to all who had heard and obeyed the call of the Lord. The converts are therefore variously described in the gospel; they were fish who had been miraculously caught (*St. John* xxi. 3–14); they were sheep who needed pastoral care (*St. John* xxi. 15–17); they were men who, like Lazarus, had passed from death to life (*St. John* xi. 25, 43, 44), or who, like the man born blind, had passed from blindness to sight (*St. John* ix. 5–7, 39–41).

This community of the true worshippers of God was for St. John unique, because it had been brought into being by the only begotten Son of God, and because it possessed unbroken contact with him, and therefore with the Father. He wrote his gospel primarily in order that men might believe that Jesus is the Son of God, so that believing they might have life in his name (*St. John* xx. 31), and in

St. John a Catholic Christian 7

order to show how the original disciples had, under the guidance of our Lord himself, learnt to believe thus in him.

By means of their supernatural faith, and by membership in a supernatural but visible community, the Christians were morally purified, and were filled with a love so intense, that St. John can only adequately express the change effected in the converts by saying that they had been ' born of God ; ' and he sums up the insight into truth, which resulted from the experience of moral purification and of love, in the words, ' God is Love.' To be a Christian was to have overcome the world, to have mastered sin, to love the brethren, and to know God. ' And who is he that overcometh the world, but he that believeth that Jesus is the Son of God ? ' ' Whosoever is begotten of God doeth no sin.' ' We know that we have passed from death to life, because we love the brethren.' ' And we know that the Son of God is come, and hath given us an understanding, and we know him that is true.' (See *St. John* i. 13 ; xv. 10–12 ; xvi. 33 : 1 *John* v. 5 ; iii. 9, 14 ; v. 20.)

This simple and direct Christian experience had, however, sprung from a background by no means simple and obvious. Christian righteousness and love and knowledge were the fruits of a supernatural faith and of membership in a peculiar and particular religious community. St. John's narrative is not the

8 Jesus the Supernatural Messiah

record of the corruption of a simple teaching ; it is an explanation of the supernatural origin of a simple experience.

St. John's gospel, therefore, presumes that the Christianity of his day was ecclesiastical, sacramental, and sacrificial, and that it claimed a definitely supernatural origin. Since, however, this gospel can hardly have been written before the close of the first century, that is some seventy years after the Crucifixion, it is of course possible that the original tradition of our Lord's life and teaching may have been moulded by the later development of Christian experience, to such an extent that the actual teaching of Jesus suffered radical alterations, and that St. John's narrative reflects these alterations. Fortunately, we are able to check the Johannine narrative by reference to St. Mark's gospel, in which the earliest known tradition of our Lord's life is preserved. The evidence of St. Mark's gospel as to the content of our Lord's teaching is therefore of prime importance.

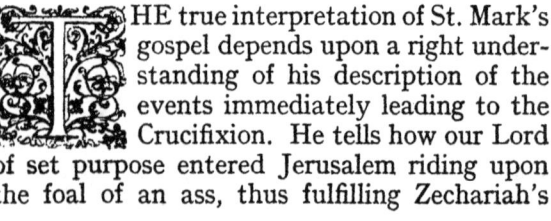

THE true interpretation of St. Mark's gospel depends upon a right understanding of his description of the events immediately leading to the Crucifixion. He tells how our Lord of set purpose entered Jerusalem riding upon the foal of an ass, thus fulfilling Zechariah's

Jesus the Supernatural Messiah 9

prophecy of the advent of the Messianic King.
'Rejoice greatly, O daughter of Zion; shout,
O daughter of Jerusalem: behold, thy king
cometh unto thee: he is just and having salvation; lowly, and riding upon an ass, even
upon a colt the foal of an ass' (*Zech.* ix. 9).
The disciples 'shouted' unrebuked, 'Blessed
is he that cometh in the name of the Lord:
Blessed is the kingdom that cometh, the kingdom of our father David' (*St. Mark* xi. 1-10).
On the following day our Lord entered the
Temple, and interrupted forcibly the prepara-
tions for the passover, in conscious fulfilment
of the prophecy in the book of Malachi. 'The
Lord, whom ye seek, shall suddenly come to
his temple, and the messenger of the covenant,
whom ye delight in, behold, he cometh, saith
the Lord of hosts. But who may abide the
day of his coming, and who shall stand when
he appeareth?' (*Mal.* iii. 1, 2).

These are Messianic acts done consciously
in order to fulfil prophecy, and the Jewish
authorities recognize them as such, as is
shown by their question, 'By what authority
doest thou these things?' (*St. Mark* xi. 28).
The parable of the wicked husbandmen is our
Lord's answer to this question. God has sent
his prophets, they have not listened to them.
Now he has sent his beloved Son, the heir.
Him they will kill, and cast out of the vineyard. As a result of this the present rulers
of God's people will be destroyed, the care

10 Jesus the Supernatural Messiah

of the people of God will be given to others, and the stone which they have rejected will become the corner stone of God's new temple. (*St. Mark* xii. 1-12.) The death of the Son will involve the abolition of the old religion and the coming of the new Covenant, of which Jesus, the rejected Son of God, is the founder and head. The old sacrificial system is at an end, for the Messiah has come, and will be killed, but after his death he will come with new power, for the new Covenant, the new Kingdom, is at hand. The narrative then continues with the terrific attacks on the Scribes, the Pharisees, and the Sadducees, that is, on the Jewish rulers. But it is not the attack of a prophet, however great : it is the attack of the Messiah, the Son of God himself.

The Crucifixion was thus inevitable. The alternative was obvious ; the Jewish authorities were forced either to accept our Lord as the King from heaven or to destroy him. The two could not exist together. St. Mark thus describes the Crucifixion as the crucifixion of the Messiah, which involved the abolition of Judaism, and the coming of the new religion foretold by the prophet Jeremiah. ' Behold, the days come, saith the Lord, that I will make a new covenant with the house of Israel ' (*Jerem.* xxxi. 31).

The account in St. Mark's gospel of the events leading to the Crucifixion is intelligible only if it be assumed that our Lord openly and publicly claimed to be the Messiah of Jewish prophecy, and that he was crucified for this reason, and not because he claimed prophetic inspiration.

The evidence of St. Mark's gospel, however, leads us further. The Messianic claim as expressed by our Lord had essentially supernatural implications.

The Messianic beliefs of the Jews were neither clear nor simple. Some expected the Messiah to come as a king like David, and to restore the glory of the old Jewish kingdom; others, that he would appear supernaturally upon the clouds, as the writer of the book of Daniel had seen him in a vision. St. Mark's narrative presumes these two expectations, and records our Lord's attitude to them. St. Mark makes quite clear that our Lord definitely rejected the first as false. The Messiah will not, he said, be the Son of David, for ' David called him Lord; how is he then his son?' (*St. Mark* xii. 35–7). And in thus criticizing this Messianic title he discarded the idea of the Messianic kingdom as a Jewish state ruled by an earthly king.

But he only rejected this expectation in order to accept the other, making, however, one important modification. He identified himself with the supernatural heavenly Messiah, who was to come in glory upon the clouds, and he described himself as the Son of Man, a veiled and mysterious phrase sug-

12 Jesus the Supernatural Messiah

gesting to those who remembered the passage in the book of Daniel a heavenly person in human form. ' I saw in the night visions, and behold, there came with the clouds of heaven one like unto a son of man, and he came even unto the Ancient of days, and they brought him near before him. And there was given him dominion, and glory, and a kingdom, that all the peoples, nations, and languages should serve him: his dominion is an everlasting dominion, which shall not pass away, and his kingdom that which shall not be destroyed ' (*Dan.* vii. 13, 14).

It was with this form of the Messianic expectation that our Lord definitely identified himself. His answer to the high priest's question at the trial was quite explicit on this point. ' Art thou the Christ, the Son of the Blessed ? And Jesus said, I am: and ye shall see the Son of Man sitting at the right hand of power, and coming with the clouds of heaven. And the high priest rent his clothes ' (*St. Mark* xiv. 61, 62). This identification is presumed throughout the gospel of St. Mark. In virtue of his claim to be the Son of Man our Lord forgave the sins of the man sick of the palsy, and overrode the Jewish regulations about the Sabbath. (*St. Mark* ii. 10, 28.)

For the reader the main interest of the earlier part of St. Mark's narrative is directed towards the moment when one of the disciples

Jesus the Supernatural Messiah 13

recognizes who their master really is. At first only the evil spirits know him; but he cannot accept their recognition. (*St. Mark* i. 24, 34; v. 7.) The crowds accept him as a divinely inspired teacher and worker of miracles (*St. Mark* i. 22, 27, 28), and the Scribes and Pharisees are puzzled by his mysterious words and actions (*St. Mark* ii. 6, 7). At last St. Peter makes the great confession for which the reader has been waiting: 'Thou art the Christ' (*St. Mark* viii. 27-29).

It is at this point in the narrative that our Lord's significant addition to the Jewish expectation of the coming of the supernatural Messiah is emphasized. The Son of Man must suffer and be put to death. That is to say, the Son of Man, who will ultimately come in glory, has first come in humiliation, veiled as a man and as a prophet, and he must be handed over to suffering and death; for only through the complete humiliation of the Son of Man can the new Covenant be established with men. It was not enough for St. Peter to recognize him as the Messiah, not even enough for him to see his heavenly glory at the Transfiguration, he had to learn the significance and necessity of the Crucifixion; and when he rejects the idea of the passion and death of the Son of Man, our Lord without hesitation identifies him with Satan, since by his lack of insight he is thwart-

14 The Church He Founded

ing the plan of God for the salvation of the world. (*St. Mark* viii. 30–33 ; compare ix. 31, 32 ; x. 45.)

WHEN once the purpose of our Lord's life and death, as recorded in St. Mark's gospel, is understood, the mystery which surrounds his person is found to be extended so as also to surround his disciples who followed him and were led to believe in him. They, and they only, are within the Kingdom, and they are appointed to proclaim the gospel upon which the purification of the world depends ; they are 'the others' of the parable of the wicked husbandmen, into whose care the vineyard of the people of God is to be committed. In them the sovereignty of God is effective, because, believing in the Son of Man, and having left all to follow him, they are the Kingdom of God on earth. The mission to the world is placed in their hands, and it is they who alone can stand upright and blameless before the Son of Man, when he comes again in glory. For the present, however, they share in his humiliation. The mystery of the elect is as great as the mystery of the Lord himself.

'But take ye heed unto yourselves: for they shall deliver you up to councils: and in synagogues ye shall be beaten ; and before

The Church He Founded

governors and kings shall ye stand for my sake, for a testimony unto them. And the gospel must first be preached unto all nations. And when they lead you to judgement, and deliver you up, be not anxious beforehand what ye shall speak: but whatsoever shall be given you in that hour, that speak ye: for it is not ye that speak, but the Holy Ghost.' 'And ye shall be hated of all men for my name's sake: but he that endureth to the end, the same shall be saved.' 'And then shall they see the Son of Man coming in clouds with great power and glory. And then shall he send forth the angels, and shall gather together his elect from the four winds, from the uttermost part of the earth to the uttermost part of heaven' (*St. Mark* xiii. 9-11, 13, 26, 27).

It is now possible to understand the motive which led our Lord to choose from his disciples twelve to be apostles, who should possess peculiar authority. They were to be the patriarchs of the new Israel and the rulers of the new Covenant. Just as the old Israel under the old Covenant had looked back with reverence to its twelve patriarchs, so the new Israel was to possess its sacred twelve. (*St. Mark* iii. 14-19.)

If then, according to St. Mark's narrative, it was the expressed purpose of our Lord to establish by his life and death the new Covenant of the new Israel, which was to remain

16 The Church He Founded

operative until his second coming in glory; and if, by entrance into this Covenant, men were to be prepared for his coming by sharing in his humiliation, we have in our hands the true interpretation of the narrative of the Last Supper.

By the death of our Lord the sacrifice was made and offered, which caused the animal sacrifices of the Temple to be inadequate and unnecessary. He was, as St. John tells us, the true passover Lamb. By this sacrifice made once and for all the new Covenant was not only brought into being, but was provided with a new sacrificial worship. In the words of institution our Lord interpreted his death as the sacrifice of the new Covenant—' This is my blood of the Covenant, which is being poured out for many '—and he initiated his disciples into the new rite by means of which they might share in his sacrifice. ' And as they were eating, he took bread, and when he had blessed, he brake it, and gave to them, and said, Take ye: this is my body. And he took a cup, and when he had given thanks he gave to them: and they all drank of it ' (*St. Mark* xiv. 22-24).

By these words and by these actions worship based upon animal sacrifice was abolished within Christianity, not by the abolition of sacrificial worship, but by the substitution of the perfect for the imperfect sacrificial worship of God. This new worship is the ' worship in

The Church He Founded 17

spirit and in truth' of St. John's gospel. St. Mark does not, it is true, record the definite command that our Lord's disciples are to continue to do this in memory of him; but it is presumed that this is intended, for, as St. Mark adds, our Lord told them that he himself would no more drink of the fruit of the vine, until that day when he would drink it new in the Kingdom of God (*St. Mark* xiv. 25). The disciples will, however, as St. Paul says, continue to proclaim the Lord's death 'till he come' (1 *Cor.* xi. 26). There will come a day when the sacrament of his death and humiliation shall itself be superseded by the Messianic banquet, which will take place at his coming in glory.

The new Covenant, involving a new worship in which Gentiles as well as Jews would share, is not an idea foreign to our Lord's teaching, imposed upon the simple moral teaching of a Jewish prophet. It formed the essence of his gospel. And, in point of fact, it is only when this is recognized, that our Lord's moral teaching becomes at all intelligible.

The prophet Jeremiah had proclaimed that righteousness of the heart was the characteristic feature of the new Covenant which was to come. 'But this is the covenant that I will make with the house of Israel. After those days, saith the Lord, I will put my law in their inward parts, and in their hearts I will write it; and I will be their God, and

18 The Church He Founded

they shall be my people: and they shall teach no more every man his neighbour, and every man his brother, saying, Know the Lord: for they shall all know me, from the least of them unto the greatest of them, saith the Lord: for I will forgive their iniquity, and their sin will I remember no more' (*Jerem.* xxxi. 33, 34). Our Lord proclaimed the righteousness of the heart and the true love and knowledge of God to be possible because he was establishing the new Covenant. True belief in Jesus as the Messiah and membership in the new Israel carried with it that righteousness of the heart and that knowledge of God which Jeremiah had foretold.

Our Lord saw in his disciples the new Israel, and he therefore addressed his moral teaching primarily to them, because among them its realization was possible. Love and righteousness and knowledge belonged to them because, through contact with him, they had passed under the direct sovereignty of God. The attack on the righteousness of the Scribes and Pharisees presumes that the true righteousness of the heart was actually attainable by belief in him and by becoming one of his disciples. The fig tree full of leaves, but bearing no figs, was symbolical of the Jewish religion, and it, like the fig tree, was doomed because it was ineffective. But the old religion was superseded not merely because it was ineffective, but because the true right-

This Church was Catholic 19

eousness and the true love and the true knowledge were actually operative within the new Covenant, which he had come to bring into being.

This moral gospel seems not to have been understood by the disciples until after the Crucifixion. The conversions which followed the death of our Lord did in fact produce that radical moral purification of the heart which he had demanded. Conversion to Christianity also involved an intimate union and fellowship of those who had passed through a similar religious experience, and led to a new knowledge of the power of God. Within the Christian fellowship righteousness and love and spiritual insight were actually attained, and in the light of this experience our Lord's teaching about the new righteousness became clear. The primitive Christians did not corrupt his teaching; rather, in the light of their experience, they learnt to understand it.

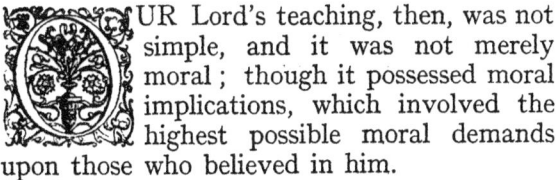

OUR Lord's teaching, then, was not simple, and it was not merely moral; though it possessed moral implications, which involved the highest possible moral demands upon those who believed in him.

Our Lord made supernatural claims not only for his own person, but also for the community which he consciously brought into being.

For these reasons we have the right to say that he taught a Catholic religion, not merely in the sense that Christianity was for all nations, but because the religion which was the outcome of his death and teaching was a religion of salvation, involving membership in a visible community possessing supernatural powers, with a patriarchal ministry and a sacrificial worship, by which was mediated the righteousness of the heart and the love of the brethren, which alone made real contact with God possible and effective.

If this outline of our Lord's teaching be even roughly correct, Catholics can confidently claim that they are the Bible Christians, and that Catholicism is not the outcome of a gradual corruption of the primitive Christian gospel, but is rather a legitimate interpretation of the life and teaching of our Lord himself.

THE CONGRESS BOOKS: No. 13

THE AUTHORITY OF THE CHURCH

LEIGHTON PULLAN, D.D.
Fellow of St. John Baptist's College,
Oxford, Examining Chaplain to the
Bishop of Gloucester

LONDON
THE SOCIETY OF
SS. PETER & PAUL
32 *George St., Hanover Sq., W.* 1, *and*
The Abbey House, Westminster, S.W. 1

The Authority of the Church

OUR conscience and our reason agree in ascribing authority not only to the commanding force which any true proposition has in itself, but also to the organ through which that truth has been and is expressed. And the organ through which we get our religion is not the individual conscience alone and by itself, but the spiritual society which Christ called his Church.

The only authority over our spiritual life must itself be spiritual. It must come from the Holy Spirit. So the religion which has the right to exercise authority is the religion which is taught by the Holy Spirit. The religion of authority and the religion of the Spirit are the same. It is to be seen and experienced in the Church which Jesus Christ founded. For it was to this Church, and to this Church only, that the Holy Spirit came with power. (*Acts* i. 8 ; ii. 4.) He did not come as a substitute for Christ, or to act as the viceroy of our King. He came to give us the blessings which flow from the risen Christ. He makes Christ present in his Church, according to Christ's own promise, 'I will not leave you comfortless; I will come to you' (*St. John* xiv. 18).

Communion with this Church is necessary for a full participation in the blessings of redemption; for the human soul has direct access to the divine Saviour, not where the soul chooses or fancies, but where the Saviour promises and commands. He specially promises his presence in three particulars: (i.) in faith and doctrine; for he says, 'Go ye therefore, and teach all nations, baptizing them in the name of the Father, and of the Son, and of the Holy Ghost . . . and lo I am with you alway, even unto the end of the world' (*St. Matt.* xxviii. 19, 20); (ii.) in worship and sacraments; for he says, 'Where two or three are gathered together in my name, there am I in the midst of them' (*St. Matt.* xviii. 20), and he gives his presence in the Holy Communion and in the union made in baptism between himself and the believer; (iii.) in government and discipline; for he says, 'Whatsoever ye shall bind on earth shall be bound in heaven' (*St. Matt.* xviii. 18); and he says to the apostles, 'As my Father hath sent me, even so send I you' (*St. John* xx. 21).

The apostles, empowered by the Holy Spirit, exercised authority in these three particulars. And the first believers continued in the apostles' teaching and fellowship, and in

Religious Authority 5

the Breaking of Bread and the prayers. (*Acts* ii. 42.) They knew that this was liberty. For liberty of conscience is no more impaired by obedience to authority than liberty of action is impaired by obedience to the laws of health.

The manner in which the apostles used their rightful power is frequently shown to us in the New Testament. One important instance is to be found in *Acts* xv., when a Council of the Church was held at Jerusalem and it was decided that Gentile converts need not be circumcised. Modern Christians may find it hard to realize the importance of this decision, but it has affected the whole subsequent history of religion. We also find proof that the apostles instituted the keeping of the Lord's day (*Rev.* i. 10), the day of Christ's resurrection, to take the place of the Jewish sabbath; another very serious decision. They taught men what they ought to believe, and how they could be saved from sin. And they had the right to expel from the Church men who taught false doctrine or led evil lives (1 *Cor.* v. 3).

When the apostles saw that they must soon depart from this world, they appointed men to succeed them in the work of founding and teaching churches, ordaining ministers, and exercising discipline. We find St. Paul handing on this power to Timothy and Titus. One of their most important duties was to

6   The Witness to Truth

'guard the deposit' of the faith and 'hold the pattern of sound words.' Timothy is told to commit this deposit to 'faithful men who will be able to teach others also.' (1 *Tim.* vi. 20: 2 *Tim.* i. 13; ii. 2.)

Early in the second century we find in all directions Christian bishops who had received this authority. The power which had been given in ordination by the laying on of the apostle's hands (2 *Tim.* i. 6) was given also by the successors of St. Paul and the other apostles.

WHILE it is the duty of the Church, and especially of the bishops, to teach the truth, it is, and always has been, their duty to witness to the old truth, not to invent new truth. The witness of the Church in the first century is embodied mainly in the books of the New Testament. The witness of the Church in the second century and in the third can be found in several important Christian writings, and in the separation made by the Church between the books of the New Testament and a number of forged and legendary books which were then in circulation. We also find an appeal made to the witness of the various churches which the apostles had founded. And then we find the

The Witness to Truth

witness of the great Councils of the Church held during and after the fourth century.

Christianity very soon attracted the attention of the heathen world and many inquirers took some interest in the life of Jesus Christ. And some of these inquirers found it hard to believe that so holy a Person had a real human nature. To us modern Europeans this seems very strange; but we find the same difficulty felt by some Eastern people at the present day. So, very early indeed in the history of the Church, we find that Catholic Christians had to repeat again and again the truth that, as our Lord truly rose again from the dead with a real human body, so he truly suffered and truly ate and drank. This is exactly what the gospels teach: and gradually the witness of the Church to the truth prevailed.

Then as the Church grew stronger, other men who had been brought up in a heathen atmosphere professed that they were Christians, but wanted to treat Christ as if he were a demigod, such as the Mercury worshipped by the Romans. They said that he was not eternal, but was made by God to help him in the creation of the world. The bishops of the Church then met together at the great Council of Nicaea in A.D. 325 and declared that Christ is truly God eternal, of one substance (not a material but a spiritual substance) with the Father. They said that the Arians, who held the other view, had no

8 The Witness to Truth

right to worship Jesus Christ if they did not believe in his true deity. They drew up the Nicene Creed which, with some later improvements, is used through the whole Catholic Church to the present day.

Difficulties were not over. After the deity of our Lord had been attacked, his manhood was once more attacked. People no longer said that our Lord had no human body, but said that he had no human soul. They argued that if he had had a human soul he would have sinned, and he would have made mistakes in his teaching. The bishops then met at Constantinople in A.D. 381 and declared that our Lord had a true human soul, as is plainly taught in the New Testament.

Then an archbishop named Nestorius won a large following among the Syrians by teaching that Jesus Christ was a human person to whom the Son of God gradually united himself. They disliked calling the blessed Virgin ' Mother of God,' because they did not really believe that God the Son was borne in her womb and on her arms. But there is a great difference between believing that our Lord is a human person who gradually became united with God because he was very good, and the real Christian belief that our Lord is a divine Person who, in his great love for us, chose to become human and pass through the same griefs and troubles as ourselves. Therefore the bishops quite rightly condemned the

The Witness to Truth 9

teaching of Nestorius at the Council of Ephesus, held in A.D. 431.

Once more there came a reaction. A monk named Eutyches was so anxious to protest against the Nestorians that he taught that the human nature of our Lord became changed into his Godhead. He confused the two natures of our Lord. Now it is plain that if our Lord's human nature was not a real human nature, his example does not really help us. It would be like a show in a cinema, in which we see people going through imaginary adventures.

The bishops of the Church therefore met at Chalcedon in A.D. 451 and carefully summed up the Christian faith, quite fairly guarding against the teaching of Eutyches and that of Nestorius. They declared that we must not divide the two natures of Christ, his Godhead and his manhood, as Nestorius had done, or confuse them as Eutyches had done.

These four Councils were the most important Councils of the Church, although three other great Councils were held before the unfortunate quarrel between the pope of Rome and the patriarch of Constantinople divided the Church in A.D. 1054. The last of these seven Councils taught that sacred pictures should be reverenced, because they help to teach us that our Lord's nature was real and not a phantom.

If we look back upon these Councils we cannot fail to see how they preserved for us

10 Limits of Dogmatic Authority

faith in the real historic Jesus Christ. The Church taught that our Lord had human feelings, that he had a human reason and soul, that he had a human will. But just as we have something deeper, something behind our feeling and our reasoning and our willing, something that we call 'self'; so our Lord has a 'self.' In us the self is human, in him the self is divine. Our self may more or less resemble that of our father. His self is the perfect eternal expression of his Father.

> Of the Father's love begotten,
>   Ere the worlds began to be,
> He is Alpha and Omega,
>   He the first, the ending he.

All the modern conflicts of Christianity with infidelity and semi-infidelity prove that if we believe the statements about our Lord in the New Testament to be true, and not in opposition to one another, then we must logically believe that the decisions of the great Councils with regard to our Lord are also true.

HAVE devoted special attention to these Councils, because their decisions illustrate the truth that the Holy Spirit has enabled the Church to teach and to explain what Christ was and what he taught. Christ has given no different revelation; and therefore

Limits of Dogmatic Authority 11

he has not given any one any right to teach any strange new doctrine, or to deny what he originally revealed. The Church could never have the right to teach, for instance, that there are four Persons in the Godhead, or to deny that the Holy Sacrament is the true body and the true blood of Jesus Christ, or to say that a man may marry a second time while his first wife is living. On the contrary, it is the duty of the Church to witness daily to the divine revelation that God is Three in One, to feed her children with that true bread of life and that true cup of salvation, and to maintain the holiness of Christian marriage. If we ask, 'Where is the authentic record of the original doctrines of the Christian faith?' the great Fathers of the Church would at once have replied, 'In the holy Scriptures.' And this leads me to say a few words about the Bible and tradition.

The deposit of truth committed by the apostles to the Church is almost entirely contained in the New Testament. With the exception of one or two doubtful sayings which some Christians believed to have been spoken by our Lord, no other traditions about him have the least scientific value. We have only a few legends which are almost certainly unhistorical, like the legend of St. Veronica. No one who has seriously studied the writings of the Christian Fathers of the second and third centuries, can fail to see that prac-

12 Limits of Dogmatic Authority

tically all their knowledge about Christ is derived from, or contained in, the New Testament.

It is very much the same with regard to his blessed Mother. For instance, the theory that she was conceived 'immaculate,' wholly free from all tendency to sin, has no support in the Bible, and is contrary to the teaching of some of the greatest ancient Fathers. Such a theory therefore, though it may be true, cannot properly be made into a dogma of the Church. On the other hand, the truth that when she was about to become the Mother of the Son of God, there was no evil in her which could be in contact with the operation of the Holy Ghost, is a real doctrine of the Church. It is taught in the Bible that she was indeed a virgin, and some of the oldest writers of the second century assert it no less plainly than St. Luke asserts it. Like the truth of the resurrection of Christ's body, it is so vital to the Christian faith that those who deny it nearly always, sooner or later, teach that Jesus Christ was a human person who might have sinned, even if he did not sin.

One of the great dangers of putting legend on the same level as truth is that it tempts those who are weak in the faith to put truth on the same level as legend. During the early ages of Christianity, the leaders of Christian thought made few mistakes of this kind. They developed doctrines simply by

Dogma and Experience

teaching old truths in a fuller, more effective, and more modern fashion. They held it to be their duty to transmit, not to transform, Christian truth. Their religion was founded upon facts—the facts recorded in the New Testament. And tradition meant the consistent maintaining that these facts are facts.

WE are now in a position to understand what is meant by what is often called 'the mind of the Church.'
The Church is not a person, and therefore when we speak of this mind we mean the age-long agreement of the minds and the consciences of the different members of the Church. Here the question at once arises, What can be the value of the opinion of very simple people with regard to great subjects such as the deity of our Lord, or his miraculous birth and resurrection? The Catholic Christian can answer immediately that the value of their testimony is often very great. The humblest member of Christ who in love and obedience surrenders to his guidance, becomes a channel of his truth. His knowledge of Christ is a living experience. He knows our Lord as his own Lord, sinless and living, mighty to save.

So St. Paul, a man of the keenest intellect,

14 Dogma and Experience

says, 'God hath chosen the foolish things of the world to confound the wise; and God hath chosen the weak things of the world to confound the things which are mighty' (1 *Cor.* i. 27). This great fact helps us to understand that the authority of the Church is not a separate thing, sharply distinct from, or opposed to, the authority of the mind and conscience of any ordinary member of the Church.

The mind of the expert is also necessary. The theologian can learn from the child; but the child also needs the theologian who has specially studied the meaning and the history of the Christian revelation. St. Paul, like our Lord himself, teaches us that 'the wise and prudent,' who think they know, are sometimes more foolish than babes in Christ: but he also says, 'To one is given by the Spirit the word of wisdom; to another the word of knowledge by the same Spirit' (1 *Cor.* xii. 8).

But, it may be said, the experts, the theologians, often disagree. Well, the wisest physicians often disagree, but their agreement is vastly greater than their disagreement, or no human diseases would ever be alleviated. And so the agreement of the theologians of the Church is vastly greater than their disagreement. The action of the Holy Spirit has not removed all imaginable difficulties from our path, but it has most certainly secured us

Dogma and Experience 15

against the errors which are destructive of the Christian life. Some things remain open questions; the Church as a whole has not decided through her bishops and her theologians every minute point of doctrine; and with regard to such things we can be content to 'know in part' (1 *Cor.* xiii. 9).

The Catholic Church has never made a dogma out of opinions which have not been in agreement with the knowledge and experience of Catholic Christians. Consider the great and serious fact of Sin, the removal of which is one of the great purposes for which the Church exists. Consider whether experience does not there verify dogma. The Church teaches, not, as many Protestants once taught, that man is 'wholly inclined to all evil,' but that he inherits from his origin a defect and a tendency towards evil. It teaches that there is such a thing as deadly sin, which separates us from God, who is the source of all our life. It teaches that forgiveness and peace may be gained by the repentant sinner from Christ through the Church. It teaches that progress in overcoming sin can be gained by union with Christ. It teaches that Christ was sinless, for he who enables all others to overcome, was himself the victor over sin; the effect has a cause.

In these short sentences a vast quantity of Christian doctrine has been summarized. But even those who have little time for the study

16 Dogma and Experience

of doctrine can see that it corresponds with experience. The Church's wisdom is therefore justified by the experience of her children. Her authority gives to us a definite guidance, a clear lead. It does not, indeed, lead us like men who are blindfold. But if we make it our real rule of life, gladly and intelligently, we shall in Christ see that light of life which all his people have followed, and other men will see his light in us.

THE CONGRESS BOOKS: No. 14

THE USE
OF CREEDS

F. H. BRABANT
Fellow of Wadham College, Oxford,
Examining Chaplain to the Bishop
of Ripon

LONDON
THE SOCIETY OF
SS. PETER & PAUL
32 *George St., Hanover Sq., W.* 1, *and*
The Abbey House, Westminster, S.W. 1

The Use of Creeds

AT first sight there seem to be two questions which ought to be kept carefully apart. The first would be, What is the use of creeds? How far is an authoritative form of belief necessary to the well-being of the Church? The second would be, What is the use of the creeds? How far are the historical and traditional forms of belief still satisfactory?

In theory, there seems no reason why a person should not answer the two questions differently; why a man should not be a fanatic for creeds in general, and a fierce opponent of the orthodox creeds in particular. In theory, there seems no reason why Christian Science or Theosophy should not have their formal statements of belief. Even Materialism, Agnosticism, or Atheism might inspire their followers to construct definitions. Indeed we do speak vaguely of a scientist's 'confession of faith' in his own science; and William James tells us of an enthusiastic atheist who 'worshipped no-god.'

But when we quit theory for fact, we find

Why the Catholic Creeds Arose 3

that this is not what happens. There are no real rivals to the creeds of Christendom. The people who find them stumbling-blocks usually object quite as much to the very existence of creeds as to what they contain. It is true in general to say that the further we get from the main stream of Christian tradition, the less we find creeds in actual use, and once out of sight of that, they practically disappear.

We might try to account for this in two ways. Either we might say that the forms of opinion most recalcitrant to credal expression were largely negative and critical, and that no one can create an inspiring creed out of clauses which begin, ' I do not believe ' : or we might say that the people who hold such opinions do not tend to form communities, and therefore do not need such symbols either as tests of membership or as corporate acts of devotion. Both these explanations are true, as far as they go : but they do not cover the whole ground. The main reason why we are justified in saying that the use of creeds means in practice the use of the historical creeds, is that creeds are an invention of Christianity.

Among the Jews creeds were not required. Even after they had lost their civil independence, they only cherished the more fervently their sense of being ' the chosen people ' of God. Politically, indeed, they were lost in the great and unsympathetic Roman Empire ; but as ' sons of Abraham ' they could make

4 Why the Catholic Creeds Arose

the proud boast, 'We have never been in bondage to any man' (*St. John* viii. 33). They were held together by no creed, but by such practices as circumcision, and the keeping of the Sabbath and the festivals, and by their special customs in regard to food—tests so rigid, that orthodoxy for a Jew seemed not so much believing, as belonging to a nation.

In the Gentile world at the time of our Lord, we find three prominent forms of 'religion,' though the word has to be used rather loosely to cover them all. First there was the growing worship of the Emperor: this was mainly a political bond, and does not concern us much. No creed was imposed in connexion with it: to treat the Caesar as a God was rather a compliment than a religious act. The incense thrown on his altar was meant as a test of loyalty to the Empire, and had no connexion with any one's personal convictions about the spiritual world.

The second and far more important type of religion was practised in the Mystery Fellow ships, where again the bond was not a creed, but the fact of having taken part in the same ceremonies, which often included the par taking of a 'sacramental' meal.

The third type hardly involves a community and can hardly be called a religion, but it has an importance in connexion with the origin of creeds: I mean the systems and beliefs of the philosophic schools. Though here, again

Why the Catholic Creeds Arose

there were no creeds, the followers of a teacher would be informally grouped together. The statements and lectures of the master would tend to be treated as 'canonical.' In this vague sense the dialogues of Plato would be 'the scriptures' of the Platonist, and the lectures of Epictetus embody 'the creed' of certain Stoics.

Now the break with the Jews 'cut the Church off from its base at Jerusalem.' St. Paul and the other apostles had refused to allow it to become a mere group of dissenters from Jewish orthodoxy: they had taken the risk of dropping the old national tie with its circumcision and festivals. Hence nationality failed to make any bond of union for the Church. Nor did political unity provide one: Christianity could still less be identified with the Roman Empire than it could with the Jewish nation. And if we ask, why then was not the sacramental brotherhood of the Eucharist enough as a centre of Church unity, like the corresponding rites in the mystery religions, the answer is, that the Church was the accredited witness to something that had actually happened, to certain historical facts that had been seen and handled.

If we consider, as a contrast with Christianity, Apuleius' description of his initiation into the Mysteries of Isis, two things strike us at once. First, that he beheld secrets which could not lawfully be repeated to the

6 Why the Catholic Creeds Arose

uninitiated : secondly, that he was shown some merely symbolical performance, a 'drama' cunningly stage-managed by the priests. But he was never in touch with history : he had no confession of faith, for he was not a witness to anything that had ever happened on this earth—only to certain supposed secrets about the supernatural world. In the mystery religions, indeed, the crowd was taught the stories of Osiris and of Mithras ; but it did not matter if they were true or not, and intelligent people merely understood them as parables. The Church, on the other hand, began by consisting of Jews, men who were convinced that God acted in the full light of history, plain for every one to see. 'God is my king of old : the help that is done upon earth he doeth it himself.' And for the Christian, this had culminated in one great act, the saving life and work of the Messiah.

So for him the Eucharist was not a mere symbolic act by which the initiated were let into the secret of some distant demigod : it was a rite founded by a divine Master, who had been seen and known, to perpetuate his presence and power. Creeds were necessary, because, in contrast to the Gentile faiths, and more intensely than the Jews, the Christian Church asserted the supreme necessity of belief in something that had happened. So St. Paul, in one of the earliest descriptions of a Christian Eucharist, clearly connects it up

Witness to 'Saving' Facts

with the facts to which he was a witness. 'For I have received of the Lord, that which also I delivered unto you, that the Lord Jesus, the same night that he was betrayed, took bread' (1 *Cor.* xi. 23).

THE creeds then emerged as an act of personal assent to a tradition of faith. But when we pass from the Apostle's Creed to the Nicene Creed, we pass in some degree from mere fact to the interpretation of fact. The most famous example, of course, is the adoption of the 'unscriptural' word 'homoousios' (that Christ is 'of one substance with' the Father). Hitherto the Church, content with the Pauline language, had called our Lord 'the Son of God.' But the subtle Alexandrian heretics found difficulties in so simple a relation as that of Father and Son. Arians stood in the streets and asked passers-by: 'Have you ever heard of a father who did not exist before his son? He that is begotten must come after him that begets. There must have been a time before the Son of God was created.'

It was in answer to this misuse of simple terms that the Church was forced most reluctantly to adopt more complicated ones. The Church was only concerned to assert that Christ was really God in a sense that no other

8 Witness to 'Saving' Facts

man could be. If she was wrong, of course the terms she used fall to the ground. If she was right, what could she do but use the current language of the day? She was not trying to invent new doctrine, but to safeguard old fact.

So, if we are told that the creeds call for revision, the question arises: Do we merely need new language to express the old idea, or do we think the idea itself out of date? Have we a better way of saying that Christ is God, than of saying that he is the same as God? or do we believe that he 'became God,' or is divine only in the sense that we all may be? There is all the difference in the world between expressing ancient truth in terms of modern thought, and dressing up modern ideas in the ancient language. One is development: the other repudiation. One is revision in the sense of a 'Revised' version of the Bible: the other is revision in the sense that a man is said to 'revise' the beliefs of a life-time. The view that Christian 'progress' involves an indefinite series of new statements of belief would make us need to alter an old text and represent our Lord as saying, 'Heaven and earth will never pass away, but my words will be revised, from time to time, as need arises.'

The creeds then, as distinct from the promises of salvation in the gospel, show the Church not only recording facts, but inter-

Witness to 'Saving' Facts

preting them by her living and growing experience. She never became on the one hand a mere chronicler of fact that had once happened (and so Christianity was never 'a Religion of a Book'); nor yet, on the other hand (as some of the speculative Greeks would have wished) did she launch out into the air and build speculative intellectual systems to account for the universe. She valued, not facts for their own sake, nor theories for their own sake, but the facts of history as implying certain beliefs about the universe. From this point of view, even the epistles of the New Testament partake partly of the nature of gospels, partly of the nature of creeds, because they themselves abound in interpretations set upon the plain gospel facts. Behind both Bible and creeds lies the spoken tradition of Christianity, expressing itself in both these different ways.[1]

The doctrinal use of the creeds then is to place before every member of the Church, for his or her personal assent, the statement of certain historical 'saving' facts, as interpreted by the Church.

[1] Before passing on it may be well to point out that this pamphlet is necessarily not concerned with the question whether the Catholic Church was and is justified in her interpretation of the gospel facts, and in ascribing to that interpretation the importance she does. It only aims at showing how the Creeds form an integral part of her attitude as teacher. For the wider question the reader is referred to Dr. Gore's treatment of the whole subject in his book *Belief in Christ*.

10 The Creeds in Worship

WE have now to consider certain secondary uses—three manners in which the Church brings the creeds before her members. Their public use has two aspects: one positive, their part in the worship of the society—their liturgical use; the other negative—their disciplinary use as tests of membership. They have also a private, or devotional, use.

Their liturgical use is bound up with the belief that Christ meant to found a society meant to include all mankind. They are rightly called Catholic, that is universal. If such a conception has to our ears a ring of intolerance, it was to the early Church something in which to glory. The vision of a Church which should include Jew and Gentile, bond and free, philosopher and peasant, seemed a great and comprehensive ideal. When we think of a creed we should not think of a document to which some menacing priest is extorting reluctant signatures, or as something 'meant to make it more difficult for us'; we should rather think of a great concourse (such as the first Anglo-Catholic Congress at the Albert Hall) reciting it with one heart and voice, and the air darkened as the faithful cross themselves; or else of the swell and thunder of the 'Credo' in Bach's Mass.

Only when we have at the back of our minds some such picture of the creeds in action, can we put in their right place certain

The Athanasian Creed

difficulties born, I believe, of a very honest but over-scrupulous 'sincerity.' Sincerity is a fine word and a fine thing. But it is sometimes confused with refusal to learn. The creeds are not yours: they belong to the Body of Christ. They are not something that you make: they claim to be something that makes you. 'But there are parts of the creed I can't understand or honestly accept.' No one asks of any man to be untrue to himself; but is it too much to plead for patience and the desire to learn?

'Sincerity' is so often a relative thing. Do we refuse to join in the General Confession because we are not in the mood? Are our poor prayers less honest because they are so far from the prayers of a saint? The creed is the full and rich expression of the faith of the whole Church into which we are trying to enter. If this is to sacrifice sincerity to the good of society, then people of different temperament cannot be 'one.' Brotherhood then can only be bought at the price of disunion.

This is the place for some remarks upon the use of the Athanasian Creed. It is best treated as a battle-hymn (as the 'Gloria' at the end implies) and sung in procession. Two main difficulties are felt about it. Parts of it are thought to be obscure, and parts of it too clear. Some clauses seem spoken darkly, others with a terrible plainness.

The first objection refers to the metaphysical

12 The Athanasian Creed

setting, the paradoxical statement of the doctrine of the Trinity and of the two natures of Christ. Undoubtedly they present the creed on its intellectual, not on its ethical side : it has always interested and often satisfied philosophers. 'But the congregation knows no philosophy.' It is very English to regard philosophy as a remote and tiresome study for specialists, but it is curious that people who are always criticizing the Church for having no intellectual background, should be the first to mock when she tries to present it to them. It is well that the many should realize at stated intervals that people have been helped by the creeds to think as well as to act. How far the Athanasian Creed can be explained so as to mean anything to the ordinary person is a question of practical exposition, with which the Church has perhaps too rarely occupied herself. But to say straight off that it is impossible, is to put a gulf between the few thinkers and the many faithful which menaces the brotherhood, and allows a divorce between faith and speculation which, in the end, is harmful for both.

The 'outspoken' parts of the creed are of course the 'damnatory' clauses, which seem to condemn unbelievers to eternal punishment. We cannot discuss this vast subject here : a word may be in place.

After all the errors in translation have been removed, the fact remains, I suppose, that the

As Tests; and as Acts of Faith 13

people who first used the creed meant by it in certain places something which many modern people find it difficult to believe. We must, therefore, ask them to concentrate on the positive rather than on the negative aspect of the truth these clauses proclaim. It is possible, I think, to say simply and sincerely that because the Catholic faith is the real and sole truth, therefore to believe it wholly is to reach the summit of salvation. If we like, we can assert the reverse side of this, and say that not to believe it is to perish; without thereby believing in 'a calendar of the lost' (which the Church has never kept) and without denying that here or hereafter, God will lead all who honestly seek him into the whole truth.

THE disciplinary use of creeds is the other—or negative—side of their liturgical use; for if to join in the recitation of the creeds is a high privilege of membership, to refuse to do so is (in some sense) to 'cut ourselves off' from the society. Our branch of the Catholic Church does not insist on individual acceptance of the Nicene and Athanasian Creeds, by each member separately. Of course public recitation implies it, but a person is not molested for not joining in. She

14 As Tests; and as Acts of Faith

requires assent to the Apostles' Creed as a condition of entry, by the mouth of the godparents, in the baptismal service, and as a condition of absolution in the visitation of the sick. Its inclusion in the catechism implies that it must be accepted before confirmation. We are, therefore, able to say that personal assent to the Apostles' Creed is a test of her membership.

A society which believes itself in possession of the truth must exact some modicum of assent from those who belong to it. No one, I suppose, would say that a person who does not believe in God, or in the historical reality of Jesus Christ, has a right to complain if he is excluded from a society that only exists because it does believe in them. But difficulties do arise when people think they cannot honestly say, for instance, ' Born of the Virgin Mary,' or ' I believe in the resurrection of the body.'

Having laid it down, as a general principle, that the Church is bound to insist on her creeds, we may add some facts that may help to modify what seems harsh and unsympathetic in such a view.

First, the creeds call for constant and careful exposition. If the Church's accredited teachers are to insist on them, a grave responsibility lies on them to see that all members of the Church know what they are meant to say. The ' educated layman '—an example to us

As Tests; and as Acts of Faith 15

in so many ways—is often a most uneducated theologian. He is the sort of person who has been known seriously to object to saying 'He descended into hell,' on the ground that it implies belief in a place of eternal torments.

Secondly, we must remember what was said above, that the creed is an ideal into which we are slowly entering. This statement does apply to the ministers of the Church, though of course with much less force than to the laity, for from the clergy, as the official witnesses to the faith and experience of the whole body of Christians through the ages, and the channels of instruction for others, a more rigid standard of belief is naturally required.

The devotional, or private use of the creeds by the individual, needs only a word. They are clearly to be used for teaching the Church's doctrine, not only to children, but regularly to the faithful ; and the faithful should help to do this for themselves more than they do by meditation on them. It has been well said, ' If we thought about the creeds more, we should talk about them less.' Lastly, in the course of our private devotion, we should say them, now and then, not as a programme to which we assent with our minds, but as a humble acceptance of truth, which we are trying to make our own more and more in our lives.

The object of a creed is, not to be abused

16 As Tests; and as Acts of Faith

as a stumbling-block, but to be used as something inherited by us all in common, and apprehended by each in his measure.

'With the mouth confession is made unto salvation' (*Rom.* x. 10).

THE CONGRESS BOOKS: No. 15

ENGLISH CATHOLICISM
AND THE
SEE OF ROME

FREDERIC HOOD
Librarian of Pusey House,
Oxford, Examining Chaplain
to the Bishop of Monmouth

LONDON
THE SOCIETY OF
SS. PETER & PAUL
32 *George St., Hanover Sq., W.* 1, *and*
The Abbey House, Westminster, S.W. 1

English Catholicism and the See of Rome

SINCE the beginning of this century the Catholic movement within the English Church has forced itself more and more upon public notice. It is not unnatural, therefore, that the ordinary layman should wonder what connexion this movement has with Roman Catholicism. Few remain, it is true, who seriously believe that Anglo-Catholic priests are ' Jesuits in disguise,' or that the whole movement is one of the dark and subtle machinations of Rome, put into motion with the object of bringing thousands into complete submission. But still the layman sees that many of the doctrines and practices of Anglo-Catholicism are apparently identical with, or at least closely similar to, those of Romanism.

He knows perhaps that Mass is offered daily in his parish church, with the full Catholic ceremonial. The queue near the confessional before the great feasts interests and surprises him; and from the pulpit he hears resort to this sacrament advocated in all cases of serious sin. It may be that he finds in his parish church all the warmth of Catholic devotion which he has seen on the Continent, worship paid to our Lord present in the Holy Sacrament reserved, and direct invocation of Mary and the Saints; and he is puzzled, because he has connected all this only with Roman Catholicism. Apart from the right or wrong of the matter, it may well seem to him unnecessary that another body should exist, not in communion with Rome, and yet in many ways so nearly resembling her. It is to such laymen as these that this paper is primarily addressed.

Now if Anglo-Catholics are to justify their existence, they will do well to show that their scheme of religion embodies that which is best in the Roman Catholic scheme, and that it has some distinctive contribution to offer in addition. Let us consider then whether this is the case. And for this purpose it is necessary briefly to go to history.

IF we look back upon the history of the Catholic Church, we find that for the first thousand years of its life there existed a great and ever-growing central block of Christians, who constituted what was known as the ' Great Church,' and there was no doubt as to who were members of this Church and who

Church of England Catholic 5

were not. Our Lord had founded the Church as the depository or 'store-house,' as it were, of truth and of power; and he promised that the Holy Spirit would lead the Church into truth. (*St. John* xvi. 13.) The voice of the Holy Spirit was recognized as speaking by means of the authoritative pronouncements of the 'Great Church'; that is to say, through such definitions of the General Councils of bishops as commended themselves to the experience of the faithful.

Now in 1054, for reasons more political than doctrinal, owing in fact principally to the rivalry which existed between Rome and Constantinople, this 'Great Church' divided into two almost equal parts; external union ceased between the adherents of Rome and the adherents of Constantinople. Then for the first time in history a serious question arose as to where the true Church was to be found. Each part of the Church claimed to constitute the whole Church, and that exclusive claim is made to this day, on behalf both of the Church of Rome and of the Orthodox Eastern Church. The matter would be simplified for us if one or other part of the Church had departed from the true faith; but as a matter of fact both adhered uncompromisingly to the whole faith as laid down in the undivided Church. Anglo-Catholics maintain that, this being so, the most probable view is that neither exclusive claim is justified, but that the two parts

6 Church of England Catholic

(externally divided as they were) together made up the true Church. If that is so, it follows that external disunion, or division in outward organization, is possible within the limits of the Catholic Church.

We turn next then, very briefly, to events in England in the sixteenth century. Up till that time the English Church had been in full communion with the pope. If we could put ourselves in the position of those who were living in that century, we should see clearly what a real need there was for some kind of a 'Reformation' within the Church. Doctrines and practices true and valuable in themselves were crudely and mechanically conceived. The memorial of Christ's death in the Mass was expressed as if it were a real death, and mathematical calculations were rife as to the exact efficacy of numbers of Masses. The sale of Indulgences regarded as magically effective apart from morality, had been for several centuries the occupation of a professional class. Meanwhile among the vast majority of those who called themselves Christians, the spiritual life was almost forgotten; essentials were in the background; Confession and Communion happened only at Easter. The nation was also grossly oppressed by papal taxation.

A reformation, then, was urgently needed; but it is deplorable that this did not happen without involving a further division in the

Church of England Catholic 7

Christian Church. It was again for political reasons that the division occurred; the final break took place in 1570, when Pope Pius V excommunicated Queen Elizabeth. From that date the Church of England has been out of communion with the see of Rome; and again we have to decide where the true Church is to be found. Is the pope's claim justified, that because he excommunicated the English Church, she can no longer claim to be a true and vital part of the body of Christ?

In order to answer this question we must apply the same test that we applied in the case of the earlier division. If it is true that neither exclusive claim was justified in 1054, but that East and West together made up the true Church, then no new principle is involved in admitting the possibility of another external division. We are not concerned to defend either the private lives or the private opinions of some of the reformers; it must be obvious to any student of history that no Christian denomination is in a position to criticize another in such respects. We may frankly admit that reforming zeal was often allowed to go to regrettable lengths, and that many influential people within the Church held unorthodox opinions. We have referred above to some of the abuses which were rife, and violent reaction was not unnatural. But the whole point is this: did the Church of England repudiate any part of the faith of the undivided

8 Church of England Catholic

Church ? Or did she definitely and unequivocally retain the essentials of Catholicism, those fundamentals which historians show us were the distinguishing features of the 'Great Church' before the first great schism ?

We may answer this question in the words of Dr. Gore (*Catholicism and Roman Catholicism*, p. 44). 'There seems to have been a special providence in the form which the Reformation and the repudiation of the Roman authority took in England. Here the appeal to Scripture . . . was joined with a conservative retention of the three great elements of Catholic unity; the Catholic creeds, the sacramental system, and the apostolic succession of the ministry.' If we read the Prayer Book and other such documents, we find that the Church of England unquestionably claims continuity with the Church of the ages, and though we miss much which we desire to restore of the warmth and beauty of Catholic devotion, we find that our communion has been providentially preserved from being officially committed to heresy. The contrast in this respect between the Church of England and other reformed bodies is significant. We realize that the full practice of Catholicism was largely dormant for three centuries, but even during those dark days Catholicism—though in an attenuated form—continued to be practised by a 'faithful remnant,' which was at some periods more numerous than at others.

Church of England Catholic 9

Ninety years ago a great movement started in Oxford, the object of which was not to introduce innovations in doctrine or practice, but to restore the true character of the English Church. The success of this movement must surely be beyond the most sanguine expectations of its originators. Such success is hard to explain unless the movement is inspired by the Holy Spirit.

At the heart of the movement is no mere question of externals—of candles and vestments and incense, as some suppose. It has effected a real and vital religious revival in this country ; even the parishes least sympathetic towards it have been greatly affected by it ; few churches now remain, for instance, in which Holy Communion is not celebrated at least on Sundays and great feasts. But this point need not be laboured, because an elementary knowledge of history reveals the contrast between the state of the English Church to-day and its state ninety years ago. The Church is still accused, it is true, of 'failing,' of not being in touch with the 'modern mind' ; but few would be bold enough to assert that it fulfilled that function more adequately at the beginning of the nineteenth century. The success of the Catholic Revival is such that, though its duration has been comparatively so short, probably one-third of the clergymen in Britain to-day are in sympathy with it : and Catholics are recognized even by the secular press as forming one of the strongest and most 'alive' sections in the Church.

THE foregoing historical sketch may have helped towards an understanding of the present position of the Church of England. We go on to inquire what definite advantage there is for those who desire to live the Catholic life, in belonging to this body, rather than in making their individual submissions to the pope.

(*a*) In the first place, it is clear that Anglicans are in a strong position with regard to the all-important problem of reunion. The fact that she has retained the Catholic essentials, and at the same time makes no exclusive claim to constitute the whole Church, has caused many to look to the Church of England as a hopeful medium in the process of reuniting Christendom.

To this it may be objected that the Roman Church has officially repudiated the validity of Anglican ordinations, and asserts that our priests are no true priests and our sacraments are powerless to convey grace; and that until lately they have additionally asserted that we alone, out of the whole of Christendom, believe in the validity of our own Orders. We

Reasons for Independence 11

cannot go deeply into this question in an essay of this length, but the following facts speak for themselves. In 1922, after very careful and lengthy investigation, the authorities of the patriarchal see of Constantinople officially asserted the validity of our Orders. The Patriarch of Jerusalem and his Synod have since followed suit; and there is every hope that the remaining Eastern patriarchs will shortly do the same. Other non-papal Catholics in Europe agree.

It is true that in 1896 the Roman Catholic Church officially repudiated our Orders, chiefly on the ground that, at the Reformation, the intention of the Church of England ceased to be to ordain priests in the Catholic sense of that word. Mr. Wilfrid Knox has dealt with this charge at length in his book *Friend, I do thee no Wrong*. We may quote briefly from his summing up: 'The charge made in the Bull of Leo XIII that the changes introduced into the Anglican Ordinal at the Reformation are such that ... they reveal an intention to abolish the chief function of the priesthood ... is entirely contrary to the received Catholic theology, which holds that provided the necessary Form and Matter are employed, with the serious intention of doing what the true Church does or what Christ instituted, the sacrament is valid.' This conclusion is borne out by the greatest Roman Catholic historian of this century, Monseigneur

12 Reasons for Independence

Duchesne, who died last year.[1] The weak position of those who attack the validity of Anglican Orders is indicated by the number and variety of reasons which critics find for their invalidity, and the frequency with which a former argument has to be discarded.

(b) A second point is that the signs of the times seem to be pointing clearly to the desirability of some form of non-papal Catholicism. People are beginning to see that the papacy, as at present constituted, is the result of a one-sided development spreading over many centuries. As far back as 1302 Pope Boniface VIII promulgated a Bull in which these words occur : ' We declare, affirm, define, and pronounce that it is altogether necessary to salvation for every human creature to be subject to the Roman Pontiff.' But the culmination of this, as we believe, false development did not come until 1870, when at the Vatican Council, it was affirmed that ' the definitions of the Roman Pontiff are irreformable of themselves and not by consent of the Church.'

It is relevant here to relate one of the results of this pronouncement. Fifty thousand orthodox and loyal Catholics in Germany felt quite unable to bear this new burden which was being imposed upon them ; they refused to accept this decree and were consequently

[1] His statement on the subject is reprinted at length in Dr. A C. Headlam's Bampton Lectures (pages 283 f.)

Reasons for Independence 13

excommunicated. The result was the existence of another body exactly analogous to the Church of England, holding the orthodox faith, but out of communion with the Holy See. This body of Catholics is known as Old Catholic. A similar incident has recently happened in Czecho-Slovakia, where half a million Catholics have ceased from communion with the pope. These instances (which could easily be multiplied) serve to illustrate the tendency in Europe towards a non-papal Catholicism.

The course of this one-sided development in the Roman Church is ably followed out by Mr. N. P. Williams in his book *Our Case as against Rome*. He shows, beginning from New Testament times, that a *primacy* may legitimately be claimed for the bishop of Rome, but that this is a very different thing from a *sovereignty* : for the latter claim he finds no authority either in Scripture or in the Fathers.

(c) Thirdly, it appears to us to be of the very first importance that the Catholic Church should welcome, and as occasion arises, recognize in her teaching, all the assured results of science, philosophy, and historical criticism : and this we believe that the Roman Catholic Church signally fails to do. In the opinion of many this is the very strongest count against her. Perhaps the state of affairs may succinctly be indicated in this way. The true Catholic view of ecclesiastical authority is

14 Reasons for Independence

that the Church defines a dogma because it is true. The Roman view is that a dogma is true because the Church defines it. The distinction is a subtle, but a true one.

To give one instance, in 1893 Pope Leo XIII issued his Encyclical on 'The Study of Holy Scripture,' in which the following passage occurs: 'All the books which the Church receives as sacred and canonical are written wholly and entirely, with all their parts, at the dictation of the Holy Ghost.' The whole Bible, that is to say, was positively dictated word for word by God, and is infallibly true in every kind of detail. Later papal utterances have confirmed this view. The 'Catholic Bible Congress' held in Cambridge in 1921 issued a report (*The Religion of the Scriptures*, ed. C. Lattey, S.J.) containing similar statements, though some even among Roman Catholic theologians modify the face value of this view in actual practice. In addition to all this, the Roman Catholic Church continues officially to include in its Missal and Breviary reference to such stories as that of the Holy House, which is alleged to have been miraculously transported from Nazareth to Loreto in Italy, where to this day the shrine is thronged with worshippers. This whole matter is of urgent importance, and is doing much to set the great representatives of science against Christianity.

(*d*) Fourthly, there is the question of the pope's claim to earthly sovereignty, which is

Hopes for the Future

closely bound up with the whole Roman Catholic system. To instance two points, the pope claims the right of kingship over the Papal States, which now form a part of the kingdom of Italy; and also the authority, as Vicar of Christ, to depose princes at his will. There are many Englishmen who realize the wonderful power of the Catholic religion as a spiritual and moral force, but are strongly averse from identifying themselves with these claims. This naturally forms for them an additional reason for remaining in the Church of England, where Catholicism may be practised untrammelled by claims to earthly sovereignty.

INALLY, we must briefly refer to our hopes for the future. I believe that the greatest hope for this generation lies in the reunion of non-papal Catholics throughout the world. Perhaps it is not an exaggeration to say that this is already in sight. When that is an accomplished fact, we shall be in a far stronger position to treat with the great patriarch of western Europe; and we hope and pray that ultimate reunion will be reached on the basis of a constitutional papacy. All Catholics would gladly recognize the bishop of Rome as the Primate of Christendom, if only some day he could modify his claim to infallibility apart from the consent of the

16 Hopes for the Future

Church. In such a united Catholic Church we should hope for great variety still in non-essentials. The august and time-honoured ceremonies of the Latin rite might well continue to be performed, for instance, in Westminster Cathedral for the benefit of those who preferred them, while those who had learnt to love the vernacular liturgy would be free to hear it in St. Paul's or Westminster Abbey. Meanwhile the greatest service which every Catholic can do to the cause of reunion and of truth, is to exercise the virtues of patience and charity, realizing that the Church which is itself infallible, must always be made up on earth of fallible individuals; and that to whichever communion we give our allegiance, there are bound to be unworthy members of it. And the earnest prayer of every Catholic should be for the coming of that great and glorious day when our Lord's desire will be completely realized, ' That they all may be one.'

SOME BOOKS FOR FURTHER STUDY

Williams. OUR CASE AS AGAINST ROME.

Gore. ROMAN CATHOLIC CLAIMS.
CATHOLICISM AND ROMAN CATHOLICISM.

Knox. FRIEND, I DO THEE NO WRONG

THE CONGRESS BOOKS: No. 16

ANGLO-CATHOLICISM

MARCUS E. ATLAY

LONDON
THE SOCIETY OF
SS. PETER & PAUL
32 *George St., Hanover Sq., W.* 1, *and
The Abbey House, Westminster, S.W.* 1

Anglo-Catholicism

IT is a very common objection to any expression of national or patriotic feeling that such expression only serves to foster a somewhat belligerent attitude towards those peoples by whom we are surrounded. If this criticism be extended to ecclesiastical matters (but under no other circumstances) we may perhaps need to justify and explain the apparently exclusive prefix ' Anglo ' which forms part of the title of this paper. Probably it will be enough to say that recognition of definite national traits does not imply, of necessity, excessive admiration for them, still less a desire to regard them as conferring a general superiority.

The history of the Church in England, the Church of England, dates at least from the earliest years of the third century, even if we set aside or ignore various legends which would give it a far earlier origin. And it is known that, at that time, despite the devastating effect of the Diocletian persecution in some parts of the Roman Empire, the British Church, thanks to the tolerant views of the

Augustine and the British

governor, suffered very little. In the year 314 British bishops were present at the Council of Arles. But after the withdrawal of the Roman legions and the over-running of the greater part of the land by heathen invasion, the Church was thrust back to the north and west. Wherever it could persist it became a strong and compact body, with the unity of aim and interest so natural in a harassed people. So utterly pagan was the rest of the country that St. Gregory and St. Augustine might well be surprised to find the Church still living in 596.

With the coming of St. Augustine we meet the first definite expression of what we may perhaps call Brito-Catholicism, for the bishops and priests of the British Church, cut off as they had been for long years from communication with the Continent, were following the ancient customs in matters which seemed to them indifferent, and steadily resisted the demand made upon them by the missioners that they should conform to a Roman use. For example, in the century or more since they had been driven into the wilds of the land, a new computation had been made for deciding the date of Easter. This they refused to observe. The Venerable Bede, in his *Ecclesiastical History*, gives us some idea of the mild and generous mind of St. Gregory, who bade Augustine, in matters of ceremony, select from any Christian sources customs edifying

4 British and Roman Uses

to be observed—some idea, too, of the sincere desire for peace which actuated St. Augustine, despite his unfortunate first meeting with the representatives of the British Church.

On that occasion the fact that he did not rise to greet them on their approach caused them to refuse to combine with him in missionary work among the heathen. They considered that one who was, as they concluded, arrogant, could not be moved by the Spirit of God. These lamentable differences between Catholics were still a source of misunderstanding in the seventh century. During the intervening years the British Church had steadily maintained its own position, and that it was not a negligible body may be regarded as certain, for the Venerable Bede tells us that in the monastery of Bangor there were seven parts, each containing not less than three hundred monks. But not until the days of St. Wilfrid, and his final restoration to his see, in 705, did the English Church conform, under extreme pressure, to the usages of the Roman patriarchate. Even then the supremacy of Rome, a supremacy far different from that which we find in the Middle Ages, did not press heavily upon the national character, or upon the highest expression of that character, the national Church.

Until the time of the Norman Conquest, despite the efforts of individual bishops to bring both clergy and laity into perfect con-

Native Characteristics 5

formity with the customs of Rome, English Catholicism retained a decided character of its own. And the great qualities of William the Conqueror were not found in his successors, who were incapable of exercising that control over the life of the Church which he had secured to himself. It is significant of the deeply-rooted belief in a necessary degree of freedom for the government of England, among those whose interests were bound up in her well-being, that by the time when John ascended the throne many of the great nobles had seen the undesirability of allowing the Church of England to be used as a hostage, or a bribe, between the Pope and the King. The Great Charter of 1215 provided that ' the Church of England shall be free ' : and its signing was enforced by the Archbishop of Canterbury—Stephen Langton—among the other barons.

A vast increase in the temporal power of the papacy during the Middle Ages may be held to account for a corresponding decline in spiritual things. Such power called for the protection of arms and diplomacy, and, in order to provide these, great sums of money were needed. Many English sees were held, sometimes in plurality, by foreign prelates, some of whom, so far from having the interests of their people at heart, never visited their dioceses. An impetus was given to the religious life of the country by the settlement of the friars, but in a comparatively short

6   Revival of Learning

time they and their influence deteriorated, as did that of the older monastic foundations.

It should be borne in mind that there was a far wider spread of the knowledge, both of the claims and of the duties of religion, than we can find at the present day. Men were probably no better, no more constant, in their practice of religion than they are now; but the Church was to them a very real and recognized part of life. The great abuses which were suffered abroad had little place in England, protected as she was by her small size and insular position: it may well be that a reputation of capacity for tough resistance may have served to strengthen this immunity.

THE fresh impetus given to all kinds of learning at the end of the fifteenth century had a good effect on the English Church: and such men as Sir Thomas More did much to commend the Humanist or 'New Learning' Movement. The renaissance of art and letters made, inevitably, for a quickened and more intelligent study of religion also; and the early years of Henry VIII's reign were notable for real reform—much of it effected by Wolsey. A sovereign whom Sir Thomas More could describe as 'most noble, wise, and liberal,' who, in addition, appeared to have every grace of form and mind, made

Aims of Henry VIII

a profound appeal to the patriotic spirit of Englishmen. It was not possible to foresee the gloomy close of what promised to be a brilliant and useful life, or to appreciate that that exceptionally powerful and versatile mind would degenerate into a ruthless opportunism.

The personal quarrel of Henry and Pope Clement VII, and the possibility that the Pope and the Emperor Charles might combine to flout the King, gave new vigour to the ever rankling grievance of the administrative pressure of Rome. It did not appear to the greater number of the people that vital issues were at stake. Henry was a firm, indeed a violent, upholder of the whole sacramental system. No fundamental of the faith seemed to be threatened : the sole outcome of his successful demand that the Sovereign should be regarded as Supreme Head of the Church ' so far as the Law of Christ doth allow,' was to be the formal rejection of a claim which had never been wholeheartedly admitted in England—the claim of a papal supremacy.

Had this been indeed all that resulted, there need have been no Laudian, no Tractarian revival, no need for any explanation of Anglo-Catholicism. Possibly it would be too bold to hope that the religious life of the people would have withstood the deadly onslaughts of indifference which were to be apparent so soon ; had it been able to do so, however, there would have been small necessity or

8 Henry's Character

scope for the ardent zeal of the early Methodist Movement and its outcome the Evangelical revival.

Unfortunately this was not all. Henry's character had deteriorated to an alarming extent. His intimate knowledge of theology was no safeguard against that opportunism of which we have spoken as the keynote of his character, and this urged him now to the brutal and senseless acts of despotism which were committed throughout the country on the persons and property of churchmen. Yet his conception of himself as the enlightened autocrat ensured his personal interest in and care for the spiritual state, or at least the accurate religious instruction, of his people ; as is shown not only by the ' Bishops' Book ' of 1537, drawn up at his direction and on the lines of his own ' Ten Articles ' for ' the establishing of Christian quietness,' but above all by the authorization of the ' Great Bible ' (a revision of Coverdale's and Tyndale's translation) and its setting up in the churches. The Bishops' Book and the Ten Articles were issued as representing the doctrines of the Church of England, with its appeal alike to the whole body of Catholic tradition and to Scripture.

But Henry's unlamented death left the country under the tyranny of an autocracy far worse than his, in the shape of a most unworthy Council of Regency, none of whose

Action and Reaction

members possessed any measure of Henry's knowledge or ability. The foreign Protestant Reformers were not slow to seize their opportunity: and the result of their work and influence may be found in the short-lived Second Prayer Book of Edward VI. The First Prayer Book of his reign is probably representative of the Book as it would have appeared under Henry's auspices. But this was not likely to meet the wishes of those who under Protestant influence, whether in England or on the Continent, hoped at the death of Henry to bring over Cranmer (who was largely responsible for the compilation of the First Book), and those like-minded with him, to the Protestant side.

The distressed and disturbed condition of the country, recently passed from the cruel despotism of a great sovereign to the odious oppression of a succession of feeble or self-seeking Protectors, was not likely to produce an atmosphere in which any new service-book would be acceptable. So when Mary succeeded her brother her whole personal influence was thrown on the side of the papal supremacy. Her marriage to Philip of Spain was perhaps the supreme misfortune of a sad and tormented life; but the natural outcome of her unpopular reign was the greatly strengthened position of the Protestant Reformers. England has not been the home of a submissive or easily intimidated race, and the wholesale

10   Elizabethan Settlement

burnings of Mary's last years produced a reaction in favour of Protestantism even more violent than that caused by the lurid close of her father's life.

Nevertheless, at the accession of Elizabeth an effort was made to continue the work of Henry on his own lines. But it became evident at once that the errors and outrages of the reigns of Edward and Mary, the instability and materialism of the one and the stupidity and horror of the other, had made the new Queen's task extraordinarily difficult. The position of the nation was one of great isolation, and consequent peril. If we may judge from what we know of Elizabeth's conduct she had at least an aesthetic leaning to Catholic teaching and forms of service, but to her inheritance of a powerful acute mind she did not add the intimate theological knowledge of Henry. That she had scant sympathy with Protestants or Calvinists is evidenced by the abandonment of a draft Prayer Book which did not meet with her approval or that of her ministers, and the setting forth of the Prayer Book of 1559. It was a compromise, but the Catholic note of the English Church was maintained ; the doctrines of Baptismal Regeneration, the Power of the Keys, and the Real Presence, were all to be found in it.

Catholic Continuity 11

IT was not unreasonable that the Protestant party should have supposed that James I might be more favourable to their cause and more amenable to their wishes, but they were mistaken. Learned, much inclined to the study of theology, but of a pedantic and irascible mind, he found their first approach to him an encroachment upon that Divine Right of Kings which constituted his real religion. Very slight changes were made in the Prayer Book, whose Catholic origin and doctrine remained undamaged.

During his reign and that of Charles I there came forward an increasing number of able theologians who were competent and willing to make clear the undoubted Catholicity of the Church of England, and to vindicate its just claim to be regarded as the Catholic Church in this country. Side by side with the revision of the Great Bible, resulting in what we call to-day our Authorized Version, went the labours of so decided a Catholic as Lancelot Andrewes, bishop successively of Ely and Winchester. To his great name, and those of Archbishop Laud and the theologian Hooker, may be added that of Isaac Casaubon, a Genevese Huguenot, who found himself ' an Anglican ready made, as a result of reading the Fathers,' before his arrival in England.

The fall of Charles I, consequent on the rise of the Puritan party, brought with it a

12 Evangelical Schisms

period of acute suffering for many of the clergy ; but at the Restoration of his son, Charles II, the Church was proved to be vigorous and capable of immediate action. The sacraments were administered, church buildings were restored, and the learning of the clergy became once more available and its effects lasting. To give one instance, *An Exposition of the Creed* by Pearson, bishop of Chester, was first published in 1659 and remains a standard work to this day. Further than that, when Charles II called a conference of Anglicans and Puritans to debate the possibility of bringing the Elizabethan Prayer Book into conformity with Puritan views, the conference failed, and with it yet another attack upon the Catholicity of the Church of England.

The end of the seventeenth century saw a real enthusiasm for religion, but fifty years later that rationalizing spirit which commends itself so easily had spread to an alarming extent. Under such circumstances it was not strange that the missionary zeal and evangelizing genius of Wesley and Whitfield ran like a fire through stubble, and came into violent contact with the Church system. The immediate outcome of their example was the Evangelical revival. This movement depended too much upon the personality of its leaders. They were men of deep spiritual life, with a real love for the person of our Lord, although inclined to a very decided Calvinism ;

The Oxford Movement 13

but they failed to appreciate, let alone to teach, the fact that the Catholic faith is the only divinely-ordered means whereby we may attain to the vision of God ; and so with many of their followers they left the Church.

Apart from this movement there were not wanting men who felt a profound apprehension of the indifference which prevailed throughout the country. Arnold, of Rugby, a little later even propounded a scheme for a National Church which should exclude only Papists and Jews from its membership. But a brighter day was about to dawn. It is difficult for an English Catholic to speak calmly of the devoted leaders of the Tractarian Movement. Such names as Rose, Keble, Pusey, Newman, recall to us a group of men who for piety and learning remain unexcelled throughout the Church. To the zeal and moral earnestness of Newman was added the vast scope of Pusey's sanctified learning, and it is useful to recall the warnings of Rose as to the tendencies of German teaching even in his day.

It could not be expected that the movement should not include among its members some whose natural tendency was towards Rome and away from England ; but the despairing defection of Newman, although a heavy blow and real loss, had no such devastating effect as was expected by onlookers, whether sympathetic or hostile. The courage of Pusey had been strengthened by a noble endurance of many sorrows and by the constant burden of physical suffering, and he with Keble and many others stood firm. We cannot estimate the debt which we owe to such heroes of the faith, and their successors were not unworthy of them.

WHAT then is our task who hold loyally fast to the agelong principles of the Church of England as described in this paper?
The term Anglo-Catholicism must not be mis-interpreted as a mere party badge. It marks the position of those loyal members of the Church in England who, desiring to emphasize the true Catholicity of that Church, unbroken from the second or third century, would display, to that end, the beauty and simplicity of the Catholic sacramental system. But this is not all. Anglo-Catholics when worthy of the name desire to spread this sacramental system as the means by which the conversion of the world may best be attained. The Anglo-Catholic who is true to his great national heritage desires to bring all men, beginning with his fellow-country men, to the knowledge of the love of God in Jesus the Christ, by the teaching and practice of the whole Catholic faith.

The most ancient history of our country is the history of the English Church. Even the

Comprehensiveness 15

necessarily slight survey of some events in that history which may be found in these pages, must suggest to every thoughtful mind the possibility of many divergent points of view among its members. We know that there are those whose main interest is in the fact that the Church of England is the Established Church, and who would persuade us that sacraments are symbols and no more. Anglo-Catholicism definitely rejects this unprimitive theory and insists that, in accordance with the teaching of the universal Church, the sacraments are to be for Christians the means whereby the soul may be united to God.

On the other hand we find those who tell us that we have no right to an independent life: that until the Anglo-Catholic has adopted every dogma and even every devotion of the Roman Catholic Church, he has no claim to be regarded as a Catholic. It is unfortunately true that many Christians may still be found, who believe that Catholicism implies Roman Catholicism and the ultimate supremacy of the papacy in the Church of England. This erroneous belief leads them to the conclusion that Anglo-Catholicism is disloyal and therefore dangerous. It may be useful to say in this connexion that apart from national and other reasonable objections, there is a great defect in the modern papal system, namely its minimizing effect upon a properly constituted episcopacy. While all Anglo-Catholics would be willing to observe a primacy of honour in the pope, that position could only be conceded to a constitutional pope as primate of a constitutional episcopate.

While it is very true that the conception here outlined of the mission of the English Church is gaining ground everywhere, there still remain within its fold those who do not hold the primitive sacramental system. Before there can be any thought of an effective appeal for unity and concerted action to the Nonconforming bodies of Christians around us, it is our plain duty to seek to draw near by sympathy, by patience, and above all by prayer, to our fellow Churchmen; bearing in mind that prejudice often springs from the hallowed sources of long association and domestic tradition.

We do not, we cannot, desire any exclusive position, or any expulsive action: our sole aim must be so to show forth Christ, that in the light which flows from the vision of him in his Church our own brethren may see that the ground on which we stand is indeed holy, and may join us there.

For a scientific modern account, based on up-to-date evidence, of the development of the Church of England and its place in the life of the nation, the reader is strongly recommended to consult Greenwood, *History of the People of England.*—ED.

www.ingramcontent.com/pod-product-compliance
Lightning Source LLC
Chambersburg PA
CBHW050336230426
43663CB00010B/1883